SpringerWienNewYork

D1224941

Kunst und Architektur im Gespräch | Art and Architecture in Discussion

edited by
Cristina Bechtler

Style and Scale, or: Do You Have Anxiety?

A Conversation with Ken Adam,
Katharina Fritsch, and Hans Ulrich Obrist.
Moderated by Bice Curiger

SpringerWienNewYork

# CONTENTS

# PREFACE

Ken Adam has created film sets that have gone down in the history of cinema.
His fantasy rooms have left their stamp on collective memory; they have become
archetypes instantly evoked by an icon in its own right: 007. Adam's rooms are visual
renditions of the omnipresent, diabolical exercise of power, whose mental reach still
strikes terror in the hearts of viewers today, as in the War Room of Stanley Kubrick's
*Dr. Strangelove or: How I Learned to Stop Worrying and Love the Bomb.*

The works Katharina Fritsch creates are objects that similarly hover between art
and life, generating a special aura that is more like a sense of energy in space than
an actual sculpture. Her gigantic *Company at Table* and *Rat King* make an indelible
impression on memory within seconds and their impact endures because they resist
facile conceptual resolution.

Ken Adam schuf Filmsets, welche Filmgeschichte geschrieben haben. Fantasieräume, die sich
unter dem Kürzel *007* archetypisch ins kollektive Gedächtnis einprägten. Räume, die als Bild
gewordene mentale Erweiterung allumfassender und diabolischer Machtausübung noch heute
erschreckend wirken wie etwa der „War Room" in Stanley Kubricks *Dr. Strangelove or: How I
Learned to Stop Worrying and Love the Bomb.*

Ebenso schuf Katharina Fritsch Werke, die als Objekte zwischen Kunst und Leben ihre besondere
Aura entwickeln und die eher energetische Präsenzen im Raum mehr denn Skulpturen sind.
Die riesige *Tischgesellschaft* oder der *Rattenkönig* prägen sich in Sekunden im Gedächtnis des
Publikums ein und wirken lange nach, weil sie begrifflich nicht einfach auflösbar sind.
Das Gespräch fand am 23. September 2008 in London, im Hause von Ken und Letizia Adam

The conversation took place in London on September 23, 2008 at the home of Ken and Letizia Adam. Affinities were quick to emerge. Fritsch is a great fan of James Bond, a love that she shares with many other artists -- not only of her own generation. Fritsch and Adam are both interested in generating moods; they are adepts at relying on the psychological efficacy and immediacy of images. In the following pages, we have the privilege of enjoying a meeting between two obviously intimate connoisseurs of suspense -- which is synonymous with "being suspended in uncertainty".

As practical makers of objects and visually compelling ensembles in space, the two approached one another with mutual respect and curiosity, inquiring into the concrete details of their respective crafts and giving us an insight into how they arrive at decisions and produce their work. As the conversation progressed, a concept of architecture and art gradually surfaced, buoyed in equal measure by futurist fantasies and atavistic recollections, linking psychology with life's elemental concerns.

statt. Affinitäten wurden rasch ausgemacht. Dass Fritsch ein großer James Bond-Fan ist, teilt sie mit vielen Künstlerinnen und Künstlern nicht nur ihrer Generation. Fritsch und Adam verbindet ein großes Interesse am Erzeugen von Stimmungen, das Vertrauen auf psychologische Bildeffizienz und Unmittelbarkeit. Ganz offensichtlich aber fanden sich hier auch zwei intime Kenner der *Suspense* – die ein Synonym ist für „in Unsicherheit schweben".

Die beiden Gesprächspartner haben sich als praktische Erschaffer von Objekten und bildhaften Raumensembles auch mit gegenseitigem Respekt und Neugier ganz konkret über das Handwerk ausgetauscht und dabei Einblick in die Prozesse der Herstellung und Entscheidungsfindung gegeben. Im Laufe des Gesprächs zeichnete sich nach und nach zudem ein Architektur- und Kunstbegriff ab, der ganz offen genauso von futuristischen Fantasien wie von atavistischen Erinnerungen getragen scheint, das Psychologische mit dem Elementaren verbindet.

It is hardly unusual today to have two exceptional exponents of different disciplines join in conversation but the inspiring vistas that opened up before us in the course of this exchange between Ken Adam and Katharina Fritsch were truly astonishing and delightful. When two of the most prominent and extravagant protagonists in the disciplines of film – specifically production design – and contemporary art – specifically large-scale sculpture – engage in a productive encounter, a third, albeit invisible party plays a role in the drama as well: architecture. Adam and Fritsch discussed issues that will undoubtedly inspire further reflection on the mental givens of contemporary society beyond the established discourses that govern their two fields.

It was Cristina Bechtler, who had the superb idea of bringing together Ken Adam and Katharina Fritsch; I thank her for inviting me to moderate the conversation. I am also

Es ist heute gewiss nichts Ungewöhnliches, wenn sich zwei herausragende Vertreter unterschiedlicher Disziplinen zu einem Gespräch treffen. Doch welch inspirierende Räume sich dabei auftun können, hat uns, die wir an diesem Austausch zwischen Ken Adam und Katharina Fritsch dabei sein durften, überrascht und begeistert. Wenn sich der Film, genauer: die Filmarchitektur, und die Gegenwartskunst, genauer: die raumgreifende Skulptur, vertreten durch zwei ihrer prominentesten und extravagantesten Protagonisten gegenübertreten und dabei produktiv aufeinander treffen, so spielt auch die Generalperspektive der Architektur als unsichtbare Anwesende eine Rolle. In diesem Treffen liegt Stoff und Anregung, über die mentalen Gegebenheiten unserer Zeit jenseits von etablierten Diskursen der jeweiligen Zunft nachzudenken.

Ich danke Cristina Bechtler, die die großartige Idee hatte, Ken Adam mit Katharina Fritsch zusammenzubringen, für die Einladung das Gespräch zu moderieren. Hans Ulrich Obrist für

grateful to Hans Ulrich Obrist for his indispensable help, Ken Adam for his interest and generosity, Katharina Fritsch for her enthusiastic response to the proposal and Dora Imhof for her expertise in coordinating and producing the project.

Bice Curiger


seine unersetzliche Hilfe, Ken Adam für sein Interesse und seine Großzügigkeit, Katharina Fritsch für ihr enthusiastisches Eingehen auf den Vorschlag sowie Dora Imhof für die kenntnisreiche Begleitung des Projekts.

Bice Curiger

Ken Adam, Katharina Fritsch, London, September 23, 2008

# Style and Scale, or: Do You Have Anxiety?

## A Conversation with Ken Adam, Katharina Fritsch, and Hans Ulrich Obrist. Moderated by Bice Curiger

London, September 23, 2008

Bice Curiger  There are some aspects that you share. Both of you work with the stylization of the image. You relate to reality, but you are not realists. You focus on the visual atmosphere. Katharina, you have also done a couple of images that relate to evil and the uncanny, like *Company at Table*, which might ring a bell for you, Ken.
I saw your work, Katharina, for the first time in 1984 in Düsseldorf, when you were just finishing the academy. It was wonderful – very sober, very severe, and closely related to the object world and to the psychology of that world. I think that also might be common ground.

Bice Curiger  Es bestehen einige Gemeinsamkeiten zwischen euch beiden. Ihr arbeitet beide mit stilisierten Bildern. Ihr nehmt Bezug auf die Realität, seid aber keine Realisten. Ihr stellt das Atmosphärische ins Zentrum. Katharina, du hast auch einige Bilder geschaffen, die einen Bezug zum Bösen und Unheimlichen haben, wie die *Tischgesellschaft*, was wiederum bei Ihnen, Ken, einige Assoziationen auslösen dürfte.
Ich bin 1984 in Düsseldorf zum ersten Mal deinen Arbeiten begegnet, Katharina, als du gerade die Kunstakademie abgeschlossen hattest. Sie waren toll – sehr nüchtern,

Ken Adam    I don't know really. I like Katharina's work, the stylization and the severity. When I try to get away from reality as a film designer, there is a purpose in it. Imitating reality in films can be very easy for me but very dull for the cinema-going audience. But creating my own reality has proved to be very successful as a rule. For example, Fort Knox in *Goldfinger* was like a cathedral of gold, 60 feet high. And then, after the film came out, the distributors wondered how it was possible for an English film unit to be allowed inside Fort Knox. It was completely crazy. Actually, if you go back to the 20s and 30s, there are Hollywood pictures, by Gibbons for instance, with these fantastic Art Deco buildings and interiors with women dressed by Balenciaga and men in black tails – completely unreal, but it was escapism for the cinema-going audience. It was the same when Alex Trauner, Billy Wilder's brilliant production designer, built a stylized version of Paris in a Hollywood sound stage. There was a certain amount of criticism that it is not like Paris at all. They created their own reality. But with Katharina, it is a stylization, often a grim stylization, but fascinating at the same time.

streng und mit einem direkten Bezug zur Objektwelt und zur Psychologie dieser Welt. Vielleicht ist das eine weitere Gemeinsamkeit.

Ken Adam    Ich weiß nicht recht. Ich mag Katharinas Kunst, das Stilisierte und Strenge. Wenn ich als Film-Designer von der Realität wegzukommen versuche, dann mache ich das ganz zielgerichtet. Die Realität in Filmen zu imitieren, wäre für mich unter Umständen sehr leicht, aber sehr langweilig für das Kinopublikum. Dagegen hat es sich in der Regel als äußerst erfolgreich erwiesen, eine eigene Realität zu erschaffen. So war etwa Fort Knox in *Goldfinger* wie eine Kathedrale aus Gold, 18 Meter hoch. Und als der Film herauskam, wunderten sich die Verleiher, dass eine englische Filmcrew im Innern von Fort Knox drehen durfte. Es war komplett verrückt. Wenn man in die Zwanziger- und Dreißigerjahre zurückgeht, gibt es tatsächlich Hollywoodfilme, von Gibbons etwa, mit diesen phantastischen Bauten und Inneneinrichtungen im Art-deco-Stil, mit Frauen in Balenciaga-Kleidern und Männern im Frack – völlig unrealistisch, aber es war eine Fluchtmöglichkeit für das Kinopublikum. Dasselbe gilt für die stilisierte Version von Paris, die Billy Wilders brillanter Production Designer, Alex Trauner, in einem Hollywood-Studio aufbaute. Es gab einige Kritik, es sehe überhaupt nicht aus wie Paris. Sie schufen eben ihre

Katharina Fritsch   When the idea for this publication came up, I was thrilled because I'm such a Bond fan. I think I've seen *Dr. No* twenty times and *Dr. Strangelove,* too. There was a little cinema in Düsseldorf in the early 80s where we went to see a Bond film every week. They showed *Dr. No, Thunderball, You Only Live Twice, Diamonds Are Forever* … all your films. It was like a cult. I just love your films and so I really wanted to be part of this discussion, but then I thought, what do we have in common? You mention the 20s, which makes me think of Fritz Lang, of German Expressionism and Bauhaus architecture. That might be common ground. We are both dealing with pictures – of course, you are much more popular, everybody knows James Bond – but our work is about creating or evoking the collective pictures that are in people's minds. That's our lowest common denominator. But I think there is also a form of a stylization in your work. I read a book about you, in which you mention that you reduce your colours. I do that too. For example, you make a room black – to get to the essence of the room, of its character. If you built it realistically, with lots of details, it wouldn't work.

eigene Realität. Bei Katharina hingegen handelt es sich um eine Stilisierung der Realität, häufig eine düstere Stilisierung, die aber zugleich faszinierend wirkt.

Katharina Fritsch   Ich war begeistert, als ich von der Idee zu dieser Publikation hörte, weil ich ein absoluter Bond-Fan bin. Ich glaube, ich habe *Dr. No* etwa zwanzig Mal gesehen und *Dr. Strangelove* ebenfalls. In den frühen Achtzigerjahren gab es in Düsseldorf ein kleines Kino, wo ich mir jede Woche einen Bond-Film ansah. Sie zeigten *Dr. No, Thunderball, You Only Live Twice, Diamonds are Forever...*, all Ihre Filme eben. Es war eine Art Kult. Ich liebe Ihre Filme einfach und wollte deshalb unbedingt an diesem Gespräch teilnehmen, aber dann dachte ich, was haben wir gemeinsam? Sie erwähnten die Zwanzigerjahre, was mich an Fritz Lang, den deutschen Expressionismus und die Bauhaus-Architektur erinnert. Das könnte eine Gemeinsamkeit sein. Wir befassen uns beide mit Bildern – natürlich sind Sie sehr viel berühmter, jeder kennt James Bond –, aber es geht bei unserer Arbeit darum, jene kollektiven Bilder zu erzeugen oder heraufzubeschwören, die die Leute im Kopf haben. Das ist unser kleinster gemeinsamer Nenner.
Ich glaube aber, es gibt auch in Ihrer Arbeit eine Art Stilisierung. Ich habe ein Buch über Sie gelesen, da reden Sie davon, dass Sie Ihre Farben reduzieren. Das tue ich

Ken Adam, final design concept for the Ford Knox interior for *Goldfinger,* 1964

Ken Adam in front of the film set of Ford Knox, *Goldfinger*, 1963

Ken Adam   First of all, I love working in black and white. I developed a technique of sketching, rough sketching, which allowed me to show the lighting or the ambiance I wanted in a room. That gave the director of photography some guidance as to how I thought the room should be lit. And I always felt, if it looks right in black and white, the colour can only help, it is an additional medium, but not necessary. So most of my designs have been in black and white.

Bice Curiger   A film develops in time and what I find so impressive about the images you create is their immediacy. There is an atmosphere, a psychological momentum that is brought into play in your films as a specifically visual feature, whereas usually films have a narrative that develops to tell people what it is all about. Your use of image, of settings and atmosphere puts great emphasis on the visual and gives it as much importance as the acting or the plot.

Ken Adam   This is mainly apparent in the Bond films. You have to remember that we ran out of screenplays of Fleming novels or books, and producers depended more and more on my coming up with crazy ideas. Often, at the beginning, if I saw a way of

auch. Zum Beispiel gestalten Sie einen Raum schwarz – um das Wesentliche des Raums, seinen Charakter zu erfassen. Wenn Sie ihn realistisch bauen würden, mit allen Details, würde es nicht funktionieren.

Ken Adam   Zunächst einmal arbeite ich gern in Schwarz-Weiß. Ich habe eine Technik des Skizzierens entwickelt, eine Rohskizze, die mir erlaubte, das Licht oder die Stimmung zu zeigen, die ich in einem Raum wollte. Das gab dem Kameramann einen Anhaltspunkt, wie ich mir die Beleuchtung vorstellte. Und ich hatte immer das Gefühl, wenn es in Schwarz-Weiß gut aussieht, kann die Farbe nur noch eine Steigerung bringen, sie ist ein zusätzliches Medium, aber nicht unbedingt notwendig. Deshalb waren die meisten meiner Entwürfe schwarz-weiß.

Bice Curiger   Ein Film entwickelt sich in der Zeit, und was ich an Ihren Bildern so eindrücklich finde, ist deren Unmittelbarkeit. Da herrscht eine bestimmte Atmosphäre, ein psychologisches Momentum, das in Ihren Filmen ins Spiel kommt, ein spezifisch visuelles Merkmal. Gewöhnlich redet man von Handlung, wenn man von Filmen redet. Die gibt es bei Ihnen auch. Doch Ihr Umgang mit Bildern, Kulissen und Stimmungen betont das Visuelle sehr stark und verleiht ihm ebenso viel Gewicht wie der Schauspielerei oder der Handlung.

DR. NO

Ken Adam, sketch for Dr. No's guest bedroom for *Dr. No,* 1962

DR. NO'S *LAIR*

Ken Adam, sketch for Dr. No's underground reception room for *Dr. No,* 1962

DIAMONDS FOR EVER

Ken Adam, final design concept of the collapsible diamond satellite for *Diamonds Are Forever*, 1971

"DIAMONDS FOR EVER" (PENTHOUSE "LAS VEGAS")

Ken Adam, sketch of penthouse Las Vegas for *Diamonds Are Forever*, 1971

improving a concept by slightly altering the script, I would discuss it with the director. So it wasn't like normal filmmaking where the script is the bible of the film. In the Bond films, that didn't apply anymore. For instance, for the shooting of *You Only Live Twice* in Japan, the two producers Cubby [Albert R.] Broccoli and Harry Saltzman, Freddy Young, the cameraman, myself and the director Lewis Gilbert spent three weeks flying in helicopters, six to seven hours a day, trying to find suitable locations. Fleming was talking about western castles and you don't have that in Japan. We were getting desperate.

The pressure was unbelievable because, by this time, the producers had already decided that the film would open in about four months in 3000 cinemas all over the world. And we had nothing. We didn't even have a script. By chance we flew over southern Kyushu and found this area of volcanoes. That triggered the idea of having our villain's headquarters inside an extinct volcano. The ball started rolling and the producer wanted to know how much it was going to cost. I said, "I can't tell you, I've never done an interior of a volcano." I did a scribble, a sketch. He said, "If I give you a million dollars, can you do it?" To me a million dollars was a fortune in 1966 and I said, "Sure." Once I had agreed and they were happy,

Ken Adam    Das ist vor allem in den Bond-Filmen offensichtlich. Man muss wissen, dass uns die Drehbücher nach Romanen oder Büchern von Fleming ausgingen und die Produzenten immer mehr darauf angewiesen waren, dass ich mit verrückten Ideen aufwartete. Zu Beginn sprach ich häufig mit dem Regisseur, wenn ich sah, dass sich eine Idee durch eine kleine Änderung im Drehbuch verbessern ließ. Es war also nicht wie das normale Drehen von Filmen, wo das Drehbuch die Bibel und Richtschnur für alles ist. In den Bond-Filmen galt das nicht mehr. Beim Drehen von *You Only Live Twice* in Japan verbrachten beispielsweise der Kameramann, ich und der Regisseur Lewis Gilbert drei Wochen damit, sechs bis sieben Stunden täglich in Helikoptern herumzufliegen, um die geeigneten Drehorte ausfindig zu machen. Fleming sprach von westlichen Schlössern und das gibt es nicht in Japan. Wir waren der Verzweiflung nahe. Wir standen unter unerhörtem Druck, weil die Produzenten damals schon beschlossen hatten, dass der Film in etwa vier Monaten in 3000 Kinos rund um die Welt anlaufen sollte. Und wir hatten nichts. Nicht einmal ein Drehbuch. Zufällig flogen wir über das südliche Kyushu und stießen auf dieses vulkanische Gebiet. Das brachte uns auf die Idee, das Hauptquartier unseres Bösewichts in einem erloschenen Vulkan anzusiedeln. Die Kugel kam ins Rollen und der Produzent wollte wissen, wie viel es kosten würde. Ich sagte: „Das kann ich nicht sagen, das Innere eines Vulkans habe ich noch nie gemacht." Ich kritzelte etwas hin, eine Skizze. Er sagte: „Schaffen Sie's, wenn ich Ihnen eine Million Dollar gebe?" Für mich war eine Million Dollar

I started worrying and taking Valium because I thought, am I crazy? Can I really do it? In *Dr. Strangelove* the script was very important but again, it was created as we went along. We had a brilliant writer, Terry Southern, who had a strange sense of humour, but it was Kubrick's decision to film the destruction of the world as a black comedy – but we never quite knew where we were because we had wonderful actors like Peter Sellers, who used to improvise all the time. You could never be sure what he was going to say. If you look at the film closely, you'll see that when Peter, playing Strangelove, says, "Yes, mein Führer," the Russian ambassador, Peter Bull, who is right next to him, can't keep a straight face. The actors found it very difficult. Kubrick was very clever and a brilliant visualist, his photography was out of this world, but he also drove everybody crazy, working on an actor's performance 20, 30, 40 times, until he got the right bits and pieces which he then put together.

\* \* \*


1966 ein Vermögen und ich sagte: „Klar doch". Sobald ich zugesagt hatte und sie zufrieden waren, begann ich mir den Kopf zu zermartern und Valium zu schlucken, weil ich dachte, bin ich eigentlich verrückt? Kann ich das überhaupt? Bei *Dr. Strangelove* war das Drehbuch sehr wichtig, aber auch in diesem Fall entstand es während der Arbeit. Wir hatten einen brillanten Drehbuchautor, Terry Southern, der einen schrägen Sinn für Humor hatte, doch es war Kubricks Entscheidung, die Vernichtung der Welt als schwarze Komödie zu filmen. Wir wussten jedoch nie, woran wir waren, weil wir so wunderbare Schauspieler wie Peter Sellers hatten, die laufend improvisierten. Man wusste nie, was er als nächstes sagen würde. Wenn man sich den Film genau ansieht, ist zu erkennen, wie das Gesicht des russischen Botschafters, Peter Bull, zuckt, als Peter in der Rolle von Strangelove sagt: „Ja, mein Führer". Die Schauspieler fanden das sehr schwierig. Kubrick war äußerst gescheit und ein glänzender Visualisierer, seine Fotografie war überirdisch gut, aber er machte auch alle verrückt, wenn er mit einem Schauspieler eine Szene zwanzig, dreißig, vierzig Mal drehte, bis er alle Details genau so hatte, wie er sie wollte, um sie dann entsprechend zusammenzuschneiden.

\* \* \*

Ken Adam, final concept of Blofeld's command centre inside a Japanese volcano for *You Only Live Twice*, 1967

Set still at Pinewood studios for *You Only Live Twice*, 1967

Hans Ulrich Obrist   It's fascinating – here we are in 2008, a show on the Cold War is opening at the V&A today and we have tension between Russia and the UK again. This show is very timely and then we have your War Room.

Ken Adam   They wanted me to make a speech tonight. But I decided not to make it because it would have been too long.

Hans Ulrich Obrist   What would you have said?

Ken Adam   Various things. I was born in Berlin in 1921 and grew up during the city's renaissance with the Bauhaus and German Expressionism and the cabarets and the music and the architecture. I feel that a similar renaissance happened during the 50s and 60s in Britain. England had never had a great fashion designer but along came Mary Quant who invented the mini skirt. You had music, the Beatles, a group coming from Liverpool! There was a wonderful Irish designer, Sean Kenny, who designed mainly for the theatre. He was quite brilliant but unfortunately died much too young. And then there were actors who came from working class backgrounds, which was very unusual.

Hans Ulrich Obrist   Es ist faszinierend – wir schreiben das Jahr 2008, im Victoria & Albert Museum wird heute eine Ausstellung über Design im Kalten Krieg eröffnet, und wieder gibt es Spannungen zwischen Russland und Großbritannien. Diese Ausstellung kommt genau zur richtigen Zeit, und dann steht da Ihr „War Room", der Kriegsraum aus *Dr. Strangelove*.

Ken Adam   Sie wollten, dass ich heut Abend eine Rede halte. Aber ich beschloss, sie nicht zu halten, weil sie zu lang geworden wäre.

Hans Ulrich Obrist   Was hätten Sie gesagt?

Ken Adam   Verschiedenes. Ich wurde 1921 in Berlin geboren und bin während der Renaissance dieser Stadt zurzeit des Bauhaus und des deutschen Expressionismus aufgewachsen, inmitten der Kabaretts, der Musik und der Architektur. Meines Erachtens fand in den Fünfziger- und

Bice Curiger   When we look back at the War Room and James Bond, we find ourselves actually spanning a millennium. Those images defined an era. It was the visual avant-garde and you set the tone, the visual tone, with the suite of images that you created for Dr. No. I saw your drawings and sketches in David Sylvester's show of your work at the Serpentine Gallery back in 2000. It seems so logical for such an outstanding representative of the visual arts' world like David to present your work to a larger public. It makes sense because of the visual nature of your work – it was so contemporary; it shaped an epoch.

Ken Adam   I think I was very lucky. That was the first James Bond film and under normal circumstances, it probably wouldn't have come out that way. It was a very low budget film. We had this fantastic location in Jamaica. Everybody wanted to be there, including myself but then I knew I had to go back to the studio in London to design the sets. The director knew me very well and I said, "Terence, how do you visualize it?" And he said, "I leave it to you, provided you give me entrances and exits for the actors."


Sechzigerjahren in Großbritannien eine ähnliche Renaissance statt. England hatte noch nie einen großen Modeschöpfer gehabt, aber plötzlich kam Mary Quant und erfand den Minirock. Es gab Musik, die Beatles, eine Band aus Liverpool! Es gab einen wunderbaren irischen Designer, Sean Kenny, der hauptsächlich fürs Theater arbeitete. Er war ziemlich brillant, starb jedoch unglücklicherweise viel zu früh. Und dann gab es Schauspieler, die aus der Unterschicht stammten, was damals sehr ungewöhnlich war.

Bice Curiger   Wenn wir auf den War Room und James Bond zurückblicken, schauen wir hinter die Jahrtausendwende zurück. Diese Bilder waren kennzeichnend für eine ganze Ära, sie gehörten zur Bilderwelt einer Avantgarde. Und Sie gaben den Ton an, den visuellen Ton, mit der Bilderfolge, die Sie für *Dr. No* geschaffen haben. Ich habe Ihre Zeichnungen und Skizzen im Jahr 2000 in der von David Sylvester gestalteten Ausstellung Ihrer Arbeiten in der Serpentine Gallery gesehen. Einem so herausragenden Vertreter der Welt der bildenden Kunst wie David erscheint es nur folgerichtig, Ihre Arbeiten einem größeren Publikum zugänglich zu machen. Es ist sinnvoll, wegen des visuellen Charakters Ihrer Arbeit – sie war absolut zeitgenössisch und hat eine ganze Epoche geprägt.

I thought at that time – it was 1961 – that I hadn't seen any films that showed the age we were living in. A lot of films were still using the old materials of set construction. So I called the construction department and said I wanted every new material that's on the market. They were wonderful and nobody was looking over my shoulder. It gave me the opportunity create settings that nobody had seen before. I was also slightly crazy: it took a lot of courage because the film unit came back on a Friday and we started shooting on the following Monday. I filled three stages at Pinewood with these sets. If they hadn't liked them, I would have been in serious trouble. So it was also a question of circumstances. If it had been a bigger budget film, with everybody around, maybe I wouldn't have designed it in the way I did.

I'm sure that you appreciate that kind of accident, too, Katharina. A few days before we finished shooting, the director said, "Do you remember, there is one scene where Professor Dent meets Dr. No; we still need a set for that." I had completely forgotten about it but I had about 600 or 700 pounds left in my budget and came up with the idea of this simple set built in a sort of false perspective up on a platform with this enormous circle and grill in the ceiling casting dramatic

Ken Adam   Ich glaube, ich hatte großes Glück. Das war der erste James-Bond-Film und unter normalen Umständen wäre er nicht so herausgekommen. Es war ein Film mit sehr kleinem Budget. Wir hatten diesen fantastischen Drehort in Jamaika. Alle wollten dort sein, ich auch, aber dann wurde mir klar, dass ich zurück nach London ins Atelier musste, um die Sets zu entwerfen. Der Regisseur kannte mich sehr gut und ich fragte ihn: „Terence, was schwebt dir vor?", er sagte: „Ich überlasse es dir, vorausgesetzt du denkst an die Eingänge und Ausgänge für die Schauspieler."

Ich dachte damals – es war 1961 –, dass ich keine Filme gesehen hatte, welche die Zeit zeigten, in der wir lebten. Viele Filme setzten immer noch auf die alten Materialien für den Kulissenbau. Also rief ich die Konstruktionsabteilung an und sagte, ich wolle jedes neue Material, das auf dem Markt sei. Sie waren wunderbar und niemand schaute mir über die Schulter. So bekam ich die Chance, Kulissen zu schaffen, wie man sie noch nie gesehen hatte. Ich war auch etwas verrückt: Es brauchte einigen Mut, denn die Filmcrew kam an einem Freitag zurück und wir begannen am Montag darauf zu drehen. Ich füllte drei Ateliers bei Pinewood mit diesen Sets. Hätten sie keinen Gefallen gefunden, wäre ich in ernsthaften Schwierigkeiten gewesen. Also war es auch eine Frage der Umstände. Wenn es ein teurerer Film gewesen wäre, wo alle mitgeredet hätten, hätte ich ihn vielleicht nicht so gestaltet, wie ich es tat.

shadows. The funny thing is that I can't find my sketch of it. I've gone through all my drawers, I don't know if I gave it away to somebody. In any case, it was that set that had such a dramatic visual impact. It was minimalist. It had a chair and a copper door. You could track back to a table in the foreground and the shadows which were cast by the grill were enormously important, like a spider's web.

Bice Curige    What about your *Red Room with Chimney Noise,* Katharina, where you use sound as an image?

Katharina Fritsch    I was asked to participate in a group show at the Martin-Gropius-Bau in Berlin. When you look out of the window in the room they gave me, you see German history. You have what used to be Goering's Aerospace Ministry, the Topography of Terror where the Gestapo was located, and the Springer Building. Powerful imagery. I didn't know what to do there, so I thought of making a room where you can't tell whether it's pleasant or not. I made the walls a very cold scarlet red. And there was the sound of a chimney howling. That was the whole room: the red walls and the howl

Ich bin sicher, Sie kennen diese Art von Zufall auch, Katharina. Ein paar Tage vor Drehende sagte der Regisseur zu mir: „Erinnerst du dich, es gibt eine Szene, wo Professor Dent Dr. No trifft; dafür brauchen wir noch eine Kulisse." Ich hatte das vollkommen vergessen, aber ich hatte noch 600 oder 700 Pfund im Budget übrig und kam auf die Idee mit diesem einfachen Set, das in einer irgendwie falschen Perspektive auf eine Plattform gebaut war, mit diesem riesigen Kreis und dem Gitter in der Decke, das dramatische Schatten warf. Das Seltsame ist, dass ich meine Zeichnung dazu nicht finden kann. Ich hab alle Schubladen durchsucht, ich weiß nicht, ob ich sie jemandem gegeben habe. Jedenfalls war es dieses Set, das eine so dramatische visuelle Wirkung hatte. Es war minimalistisch. Es gab einen Stuhl und eine Kupfertür. Man konnte zu einem Tisch im Vordergrund zurückfahren, und die Schatten, die das Gitter warf, waren extrem wichtig, wie ein Spinnennetz.

Bice Curiger    Wie war das bei *Roter Raum mit Kamingeräusch,* Katharina, wo du den Ton ins Bild integrierst?

Katharina Fritsch: Ich wurde gebeten, an einer Gruppenausstellung im Martin-Gropius-Bau in Berlin mitzuwirken. Wenn man in dem Raum, der mir zugeteilt wurde, aus dem Fenster schaut, sieht man ein Stück Deutsche Geschichte: Das frühere Luftfahrtministerium von Göring, die

of the chimney. It created a strange atmosphere that you couldn't really grasp and that was heightened by looking out of the window at this historical site.

Ken Adam   What you did at the Gropius-Bau is very dramatic. When did you do that?

Katharina Fritsch   In 1991, shortly after the wall came down.

Bice Curiger   It's related to collective history, to the immediacy of symbolic forms that can be interpreted in one way and can suddenly turn into something completely different. Looking at the image of the War Room, I started to see the lamp, the ring as a Saturnian ring, which gives the whole scene another meaning.

Ken Adam   Funny you should mention that. I agree with you. I had a big fight, initially, with Stanley because we learned in the old school that the designer of the film makes a sketch for the establishing shot of the set. Famous designers many years ago even insisted on nailing a spike into the floor to force the director to shoot the establishing shot from that position. Stanley said, "I am not going to use this angle." He was

Topographie des Terrors, wo die Gestapo untergebracht war, und das Springer-Gebäude. Starke Bildelemente. Ich wusste nicht, was ich dort machen sollte, also dachte ich mir einen Raum aus, von dem man nicht weiß, ob er angenehm ist oder nicht. Die Wände gestaltete ich in einem sehr kalten Dunkelrot. Dazu kam das Geräusch eines heulenden Kamins. Das war der ganze Raum: die roten Wände und das Heulen des Kamins. Dadurch entstand eine seltsame Atmosphäre, die man nicht wirklich benennen konnte und die durch den Blick aus dem Fenster auf das historische Gelände noch verstärkt wurde.

Ken Adam   Was Sie im Gropius-Bau gemacht haben, ist sehr bühnenwirksam gedacht. Wann war das?

Katharina Fritsch   1991, kurz nach dem Fall der Mauer.

Bice Curiger   Es hängt mit der kollektiven Geschichte zusammen, mit der Unmittelbarkeit symbolischer Formen, die auf eine bestimmte Art interpretiert werden können und sich dann plötzlich als etwas ganz anderes entpuppen. Als ich das Bild des War Rooms anschaute, sah ich zuerst die Lampe, diesen Ring, als einen Ring des Saturn; das gibt der ganzen Szene eine völlig andere Bedeutung.

Katharina Fritsch, *Roter Raum mit Kamingeräusch*
(Red Room with Chimney Noise), Martin Gropius Bau,
Berlin, 1991

referring to my sketch of the overall view of the triangular shaped War Room. Stanley said that he didn't want an establishing shot that reveals the entire set; he didn't want the audience to know where they are; he wanted to make them feel disoriented. So he started filming the actors around the big circular table with the light ring above to give the impression of playing a poker for the fate of the world and, of course, he was right. We experimented in his flat in the evenings with photofloods that he held up above me to get the right angle and the right amount of light. He managed to cast light on 36 actors around the table without using any fill light. All the light on the whole set came only from the ring. That's fantastic.

Hans Ulrich Obrist   Then there was the floor, a very special floor, and the maps.

Bice Curiger   The light in the map and the little holes through which you see the light.

Ken Adam   But they were phony. We would have needed 36 projectors to project the tracks of the B52s on the map and Stanley said, "If one breaks down we might be held up for hours. I'd rather you do it mechanically." So I blew up the maps photographically

Ken Adam   Lustig, dass Sie das sagen. Ich bin auch dieser Ansicht. Zuerst hatte ich einen heftigen Streit mit Stanley, weil wir nach alter Schule gelernt hatten, dass der Filmdesigner eine Skizze für die erste Einstellung von jedem Set macht. Vor vielen Jahren haben berühmte Designer sogar darauf bestanden, einen Stift in den Boden zu nageln, um den Regisseur zu zwingen, die erste Einstellung von diesem Punkt aus zu drehen. Stanley sagte: „Ich werde nicht diesen Blickwinkel wählen." Er bezog sich dabei auf meine Zeichnung der Gesamtansicht des dreieckigen War Rooms. Stanley meinte, er wolle in der ersten Einstellung nicht gleich das gesamte Set enthüllen; er wollte nicht, dass das Publikum wusste, wo es sich befand; er wollte, dass es verwirrt wäre. Also filmte er zuerst die Schauspieler an dem großen runden Tisch unter dem Lichtring, um den Eindruck zu erwecken, es würde um das Schicksal der Welt gepokert, und er hatte natürlich recht. Wir experimentierten abends jeweils in seiner Wohnung, indem er Photoleuchten über mich hielt, um den richtigen Winkel und die richtige Lichtmenge herauszufinden. Er schaffte es, ohne den Einsatz von Füll-Licht 36 Schauspieler um den Tisch herum zu beleuchten. Das ganze Licht auf dem gesamten Set stammte allein von dem Ring. Das ist fantastisch.

Hans Ulrich Obrist   Dann war da noch der Boden, ein sehr spezieller Boden, und die Weltkarten.

to that size and we glued them onto plywood. I cut out each symbol making a little light box and put 60 or 100 watt light bulbs in them. What I didn't realize was that the lighting gave off so much heat that the photo used to bubble up from the plywood backing. So we had to install two air-conditioning units. But since it was all done mechanically, we had much more control over everything. The other strangely claustrophobic effect was created because I used a highly reflective floor. You had the maps and that black floor.

Cristina Bechtler   Which created a deconstructivist feel to the room.

Bice Curiger   Because the maps are at a right angle and then you have this very strong light on the other side. It's a little bit like Fritz Lang.

Cristina Bechtler   Or like Lionel Feininger's paintings?

Bice Curiger   Feininger is not so 'unheimlich' or uncanny.


Bice Curiger   Das Licht auf der Karte und die kleinen Löcher, durch die das Licht dringt.

Ken Adam   Aber die waren getürkt. Wir hätten 36 Projektoren gebraucht, um die Flugbahnen der B52-Bomber auf die Karte zu projizieren, und Stanley sagte: „Wenn einer ausfällt, kann uns das stundenlang aufhalten. Mir wäre lieber, du machst das mechanisch." Also habe ich die Karten fotografisch auf diese Größe aufgeblasen und wir montierten sie auf Sperrholz. Ich habe jedes Symbol ausgesägt und eine kleine Leuchtbox dahinter befestigt und mit einer 60- oder 100-Watt-Birne ausgerüstet. Allerdings hatte ich nicht daran gedacht, dass das Licht so viel Wärme erzeugte, dass das Foto auf der Sperrholzplatte Blasen zu schlagen begann. Also mussten wir zwei Belüftungsapparate installieren. Doch weil alles mechanisch war, hatten wir es einigermaßen im Griff. Der andere, seltsam klaustrophobische Effekt entstand, weil ich einen stark spiegelnden Bodenbelag verwendete. Da waren die Karten und dann dieser schwarze Boden.

Cristina Bechtler   Die dem Raum einen dekonstruktivistischen Anstrich gaben.

Bice Curiger   Weil sich die Karten im rechten Winkel zum Boden befinden und dann ist da dieses sehr starke Licht auf der anderen Seite. Es ist ein bisschen wie Fritz Lang.

Ken Adam, final concept drawing for the War Room for *Dr Strangelove, or: How I Learned to Stop Worrying and Love the Bomb,* 1964

Ken Adam    Yes, it was 'unheimlich'. In retrospect, I think it was the best set I ever designed because it created absolutely the right atmosphere for the film – and the actors felt it. That's a great compliment because it is not very often that you hit the nail on the head. Terry Southern who was a little crazy. When he came on the set the first night, he looked around and said, "Interesting set, but will it dress?" To 'dress' a set means to fill it with furniture. And I said, "That's how it is going to stay." He knew that. He was just trying to tease me.

Bice Curiger    I think there really is a connection between the War Room and *Company at Table.*

Katharina Fritsch    In 1988 Jean-Christophe Ammann – he was the curator of the Kunsthalle Basel at that time – invited me to do something for the big gallery. I hadn't seen *Dr. Strangelove* yet, but I think there is a kind of collective memory of such large companies at table – I immediately had a vision of this long, long table with 32 men sitting at it.

Cristina Bechtler    Oder wie die Bilder von Lionel Feininger?

Bice Curiger    Feininger ist nicht so unheimlich.

Ken Adam    Ja, es war unheimlich. Im Nachhinein denke ich, das war das beste Set, das ich je entworfen habe, weil es genau die richtige Atmosphäre für den Film schuf – und die Schauspieler konnten sie spüren. Das ist ein großes Kompliment, weil es nicht so häufig vorkommt, dass man den Nagel auf den Kopf trifft. Terry Southern war ja ein wenig verrückt ... Als er am ersten Abend auf dem Set war, schaute er sich um und sagte: „Interessantes Set, aber lässt es sich kleiden?" Ein Set „zu kleiden", englisch „to dress", heißt, es mit Möbeln ausstatten. Und ich sagte: „Es wird so bleiben." Das war ihm natürlich klar. Er wollte mich nur auf den Arm nehmen.

Bice Curiger    Ich glaube, es gibt wirklich eine Verbindung zwischen dem War Room und der *Tischgesellschaft*.

Katharina Fritsch    1988 hat mich Jean-Christophe Ammann – damals Kurator an der Kunsthalle Basel – eingeladen, etwas für den großen Ausstellungssaal zu machen. Ich hatte *Dr. Strangelove*

Katharina Fritsch, *Tischgesellschaft* (Company at Table), 1988

Ken Adam  It's brilliant, I love that work.

Katharina Fritsch  It's very strange. The figure is modelled after an introspective person, passive, almost autistic, maybe even with drugs involved. So I got the idea of "Ich bin viele / I am many" – a schizophrenic personality. That's what this piece is about.

Hans Ulrich Obrist  Once you've seen it, you can't forget it. It has the same immediacy that Dr. Strangelove has.

Bice Curiger  And the pattern of the tablecloth as you walk past is like a hallucination; you see the lines of the white faces almost becoming part of the red and white tablecloth. It's psychedelic.

Katharina Fritsch  When I did the *Rat King* in New York in 1993, I used wide angle photos in the catalogue, like a movie screen. I really was thinking of Kubrick; I was deeply impressed by his films – like *The Shining*.

noch nicht gesehen, aber ich denke, es gibt eine Art kollektive Erinnerung an so große Tischgesellschaften. Ich hatte jedenfalls sofort die Vision von diesem endlos langen Tisch mit 32 Männern, die an ihm sitzen.

Ken Adam  Es ist brillant, ich liebe dieses Werk.

Katharina Fritsch  Es ist sehr seltsam. Die Figur ist ein Abguss von einem Menschen, der mir damals sehr introvertiert, passiv und in sich selbst gefangen erschien, vielleicht waren auch Drogen im Spiel. So kam mir die Idee des „Ich bin viele" – der schizophrenen Persönlichkeit. Darum geht es in dieser Arbeit.

Hans Ulrich Obrist  Wenn man sie einmal gesehen hat, vergisst man sie nicht mehr. Sie hat dieselbe Unmittelbarkeit wie *Dr. Strangelove*.

Bice Curiger  Und im Vorübergehen wirkt das Muster auf der Tischdecke geradezu halluzinatorisch; die Züge der weißen Gesichter werden fast Teil der rot-weißen Tischdecke. Ein psychedelisches Erlebnis.

Ken Adam   So you built all 32 figures?

Katharina Fritsch   I had the same problems you had with money. My producers or my other gallerists thought it was a waste of money.

Bice Curiger   Sometimes you destroy a work after you've built it because you find out it doesn't have the right proportions. You can't tell ahead of time. It's not like a painting; you can't continue where you left off the evening before.

Ken Adam   You could have taken photographs.

Katharina Fritsch   I didn't. I made a model in my studio. I didn't have any money at all at the time. The room was unheated. I made a table with the tablecloth and this one figure out of wax sitting at the table. I thought it might work, so I just did it. I had only two months. I made it in time but it was a nightmare.

Ken Adam   The existing building had a parquet floor?

Katharina Fritsch   Als ich 1993 in New York den *Rattenkönig* machte, habe ich für den Katalog Weitwinkelaufnahmen verwendet, wie für eine Filmleinwand. Dabei dachte ich tatsächlich an Kubrick; ich war schwer beeindruckt von seinen Filmen – etwa *The Shining.*

Ken Adam   Also haben Sie alle 32 Figuren selbst gemacht?

Katharina Fritsch   Ich hatte dieselben Geldprobleme wie Sie. Meine Produzenten oder meine übrigen Galeristen hielten es für Geldverschwendung.

Bice Curiger   Manchmal zerstörst du eine fertige Arbeit, weil du findest, sie habe nicht die richtigen Proportionen. Du weißt es nicht zum Voraus. Es ist nicht wie in der Malerei; du kannst nicht dort fortfahren, wo du am Vorabend aufgehört hast.

Ken Adam   Sie hätten Fotos machen können.

Katharina Fritsch   Habe ich nicht. Ich habe im Atelier ein Modell gebaut. Ich hatte damals kein Geld. Der Raum war ungeheizt. Ich machte einen Tisch mit einer Tischdecke und dieser einen Wachsfigur, die am Tisch sitzt. Ich dachte, es könnte funktionieren, also habe ich es einfach

Katharina Fritsch   Yes, I made it especially for the Kunsthalle Basel because I liked the skylight in that room. It has a slightly claustrophobic character: there are no windows, just the skylight.

\* \* \*

Bice Curiger   I wonder about parallel worlds and how the idea relates to the War Room.

Katharina Fritsch   When I work I often think about the idea of meta-worlds. You've talked about making things more 'real' than reality. Meta-world or parallel world is a good word for that.

Cristina Bechtler   Like a typology of collective fears.

Katharina Fritsch   Yes, this is also what I like about the James Bond films: they invent archetypical places. For example, we might be told that the location is Jamaica. I've never been there, but my picture of what it's like comes from the James Bond films.

gemacht. Ich hatte nur zwei Monate Zeit. Ich habe es rechtzeitig geschafft, aber es war ein Alptraum.

Ken Adam   Das entsprechende Gebäude hatte einen Parkettboden?

Katharina Fritsch   Ja, ich machte es speziell für die Kunsthalle Basel, weil ich das Oberlicht in diesem Saal mochte. Er hat etwas Klaustrophobisches: es gibt keine Fenster, nur dieses Oberlicht.

\* \* \*

Bice Curiger   Ich denke gerade an Parallelwelten und wie dieser Gedanke mit dem War Room zusammenhängt.

Katharina Fritsch   Ich denke bei der Arbeit oft über Meta-Welten nach. Du hast davon gesprochen, Dinge „realer" zu machen, als sie in Wirklichkeit sind. Meta-Welt oder Parallelwelt ist eine gute Umschreibung dafür.

Bice Curiger   It's generic. I think this is also the power of images, you can invent and create. They can encapsulate more than reality itself. So what you get in such images of the world is a concentrated, distilled comment on reality.

Hans Ulrich Obrist   That leads us to Katharina's postcards.

[looking at the Modena catalogue]

Katharina Fritsch   This is what I am doing now. My work has become a little bit softer, it's my *Barry Lyndon,* so to speak. My last show in New York was a kind of garden scenario with sculptures and pictures. I call it a meta-gallery. In a gallery you have pictures and figures. If you made a film with a gallery in it, maybe you would create it like this. Now I am combining the prints with sculptures.

Ken Adam   It is quite daring for you to have such strange perspectives and that huge green image there at an angle.

Cristina Bechtler   Eine Art Typologie der kollektiven Ängste.

Katharina Fritsch   Ja, das ist auch etwas, was mir an den James-Bond-Filmen gefällt: sie schaffen archetypische Orte. Zum Beispiel wird uns gesagt, dass das Ganze in Jamaika spielt. Ich war noch nie dort, aber mein Bild von Jamaika stammt aus den James-Bond-Filmen.

Bice Curiger   Das ist ein allgemeines Phänomen. Ich glaube, dass dies auch zur Macht der Bilder gehört, dass sie uns erlauben, etwas zu erfinden, kreativ zu werden. In ihnen steckt mehr als die gezeigte Realität. Solche Bilder von der Welt liefern einen Kommentar zur Realität in konzentrierter Form.

Hans Ulrich Obrist   Das bringt uns auf Katharinas Postkarten.

[auf den Modena-Katalog blickend]

Katharina Fritsch   Das ist, was ich jetzt gerade mache. Meine Kunst ist ein bisschen weicher geworden, dies ist sozusagen mein *Barry Lyndon.* Meine letzte Ausstellung in New York war eine Art Gartenszene mit Skulpturen und Bildern. Ich nenne das eine Meta-Galerie. In einer Galerie

Katharina Fritsch, installation view
exhibition at Matthew Marks Gallery,
New York, 2008

Ken Adam, research drawing by Ivor Beddoes for Saxon Border Post for *Barry Lyndon*, 1975

Katharina Fritsch   I like the idea of making a kind of diagonal pavilion where the view changes as you walk around it, like walking through a garden. I also want special lighting to create different moods. Very light ones or darker ones.

Hans Ulrich Obrist   You both relate to architecture, too. Like what you did at the Venice Biennale in 1995, Katharina.

Katharina Fritsch   The piece for Venice was an architectural model for a museum in the scale of 1:10 – like a huge oversized architectural model for a building which can also be a sculpture. It was on a pedestal 1.60 meters tall, at my eye level, so basically you could only see it by going upstairs in the German Pavilion and looking down on it. Unfortunately, they closed off the stairs so people were confused and actually very angry about it.
It was also a kind of UFO. I like the idea of making a museum like those little glass pavilions for cars in the 50s. You can see the sculptures in it even when the museum is closed. There was a staircase inside leading to a room above with golden walls. Inside there is this space with colored glass. I wanted the light

hat man Bilder und Figuren. Wenn man einen Film drehen würde, in der eine Galerie vorkommt, würde man sie wahrscheinlich so ähnlich gestalten. Nun kombiniere ich die Druckgrafik mit Skulpturen.

Ken Adam   Es ist ziemlich mutig von Ihnen, so seltsame Perspektiven zu wählen, und dann dieses riesige grüne Bild dort querzustellen.

Katharina Fritsch   Mir gefällt die Idee, eine Art diagonalen Pavillon zu bauen, bei dem sich die Aussicht verändert, wenn man darin herumgeht, wie wenn man durch einen Garten spazieren würde. Es entsteht ein spezielles Licht, mit dem sich verschiedene Stimmungen erzeugen lassen. Sehr helle oder eher düstere.

Hans Ulrich Obrist   Bei euch beiden besteht ein Bezug zur Architektur. Ich denke zum Beispiel an die Arbeit, die du für die Biennale in Venedig 1995 gemacht hast, Katharina.

Katharina Fritsch   Die Arbeit für Venedig war ein Architekturmodell für ein Museum im Maßstab 1:10 – wie ein gigantisches, zu groß geratenes Architekturmodell für ein Gebäude, das auch eine Skulptur sein könnte. Es stand auf einem 1,6 Meter hohen Podest, das entspricht meiner

inside to resemble the light in a church. The roof was silver and the outer walls were golden, a little bit like expressionistic or futurist architecture, or some kind of exotic architecture.

Cristina Bechtler   Or Castell del Monte. We have the octagon and the pentagon …

Hans Ulrich Obrist   So you design films and you make fine art and the fascinating thing is that you both venture into architecture; you're even mentioned in books on architecture.

Bice Curiger   We live in a visual era; images penetrate our lives. I think both of you have the genius of treating images like tools that generate immediacy; we respond immediately before the intellect has a chance to come into play. In Katharina's work, the imagery is created in sculptures and screenprints and for Ken it's architecture. In Katharina's work, it is a sculpture, but it is also an image. And for Ken it is architecture, but it is also an image.


Augenhöhe, also konnte man es eigentlich nur sehen, wenn man im Deutschen Pavillon die Treppe hoch ging und es von oben anschaute. Unglücklicherweise wurde diese Treppe gesperrt, so dass die Leute wie vor den Kopf gestoßen waren und richtig ärgerlich wurden. Es war auch eine Art UFO. Mir gefällt die Vorstellung, ein Museum zu bauen, das ausschaut wie die kleinen Glaspavillons für Autos in den Fünfzigerjahren. Man kann die Skulpturen darin auch sehen, wenn das Museum geschlossen ist. Im Inneren gab es eine Treppe, die in einen Raum mit Fenstern aus farbigem Glas hinaufführte. Innen ist dieser Raum in farbigem Glas. Ich wollte, dass das Licht darin wie in einer Kirche wirken sollte. Das Dach war silberfarben und die Außenwände golden, ein bisschen wie expressionistische oder futuristische Architektur.

Cristina Bechtler   Oder wie Castell del Monte. Ein Achteck und ein Fünfeck …

Hans Ulrich Obrist   Sie gestalten also Filmsets und du machst Kunst, und das Spannende ist, dass ihr beide euch mit Architektur befasst; ihr werdet sogar in Architekturbüchern erwähnt.

Bice Curiger   Wir leben in einem visuellen Zeitalter; unser Leben ist von Bildern durchdrungen. Ich glaube, dass ihr beide die Gabe habt, mit Bildern wie mit Werkzeugen umzugehen, die Unmittelbarkeit erzeugen; wir reagieren sofort darauf, bevor der Intellekt eine Chance hat, sich

Hans Ulrich Obrist   Like your pavilion for Berlin, Ken.

Cristina Bechtler   What was it initially planned for?

Ken Adam   The curator of the Gropius-Bau offered me a space at the back of the building. We flew by jet to Berlin last March. It was all very impressive.

Cristina Bechtler   What was the purpose of the pavilion? Was it supposed to be a sculpture?

Ken Adam   I wanted to play around. People always want to know what purpose a pavilion has. I looked at Gehry's pavilion again yesterday. I admire Gehry greatly, but I don't necessarily admire his pavilion for the Serpentine. The roof is interesting. I can relate to that. But it looked much more interesting when it was in a rough state than it does now with everything finished. If you asked him what it's for, he would say, if they have an exhibition, people can have a drink there, uncomfortably.


einzuschalten. In Katharinas Werk besteht das Vokabular aus Skulpturen und Siebdrucken und bei Ken ist es architektonisch. Bei Katharina ist es eine Skulptur, aber gleichzeitig ein Bild. Und bei Ken ist es Architektur, aber gleichzeitig ein Bild.

Hans Ulrich Obrist   Wie im Fall Ihres Pavillons für Berlin, Ken.

Cristina Bechtler   Wozu war der ursprünglich gedacht?

Ken Adam   Der Kurator des Gropius-Baus stellte mir einen Raum an der Rückseite des Gebäudes zur Verfügung. Wir flogen dieses Jahr im März mit dem Jet nach Berlin. Es war alles sehr beeindruckend.

Cristina Bechtler   Was war der Zweck des Pavillons? War er als Skulptur gedacht?

Ken Adam   Ich wollte etwas herumspielen. Die Leute wollen immer wissen, wozu ein Pavillon gedacht ist. Ich habe mir gestern wieder einmal Gehrys Pavillon angeschaut. Ich bewundere Gehry sehr, aber seinen Pavillon für die Serpentine Gallery bewundere ich nicht unbedingt. Das Dach ist interessant. Damit kann ich etwas anfangen. Aber im Rohzustand sah alles viel

Katharina Fritsch, *Museum, Model 1:10*
(Museum Model 1:10), 1995

Ken Adam, sketch for a pavilion in Berlin commissioned by the Orneberg Foundation, 2008

Hans Ulrich Obrist   I don't agree. The pavilion worked very well all summer for events, coffee breaks, lectures and other public programs, park nights, parties, and last but not least a Manifesto Marathon which connected to Speakers' Corner. And early mornings, there were even joggers who unexpectedly appropriated the pavillion.

Bice Curiger   You had an exhibition at the Gropius-Bau eight years ago. What did you do there?

Ken Adam   I was working on a film in Hollywood. Gereon Sievernich, one of the curators of the Gropius-Bau, flew over in 1998 and asked me if I'd like to design the Millennium show there. And I said, "Well, show me what the Gropius-Bau is." He showed me some photographs and said he wanted a sort of Bond design. I didn't want to overpower the 19th century architecture behind it. Besides, I didn't really understand – it was a very highbrow scientific exhibition and I am not at all … So I came up with what Gereon originally wanted to do. There were two antique globes of the world in France somewhere, but transporting them to Berlin was a problem, so I said, let me do

interessanter aus als jetzt, wo es fertig ist. Wenn man ihn fragen würde, wozu der Pavillon dient, würde er sagen, dass die Leute dort während einer Ausstellung auf unbequeme Art etwas trinken könnten.

Hans Ulrich Obrist   Das sehe ich anders. Der Pavillon hat seinen Dienst den ganzen Sommer über bestens erfüllt, für Kaffeepausen, Lesungen und andere öffentliche Veranstaltungen, bei nächtlichen Anlässen im Park, Partys, und nicht zuletzt beim *Serpentine Manifesto Marathon,* der auf den Speakers' Corner Bezug nahm. Außerdem wurde der Pavillon am frühen Morgen ganz unerwartet von den Joggern im Park in Beschlag genommen.

Bice Curiger   Sie hatten vor acht Jahren eine Ausstellung im Gropius-Bau. Was haben Sie dort gezeigt?

Ken Adam   Ich arbeitete in Hollywood an einem Film. Gereon Sievernich, einer der Kuratoren des Gropius-Baus, flog 1998 herüber und fragte mich, ob ich Lust hätte, die Millennium-Schau dort zu gestalten. Und ich sagte: „Zeigen Sie mir, wie der Gropius-Bau aussieht." Er zeigte mir einige Fotografien und sagte, er möchte eine Art Bond-Design. Ich wollte jedoch der dem Bau zugrundeliegenden Architektur aus dem 19. Jahrhundert keine Gewalt antun. Im Übrigen

Ken Adam, concept for the
entrance of the exhibition
*Theatrum naturae et artis
Wunderkammern des Wissens*,
Martin-Gropius-Bau, Berlin,
1999

a globe. I did one that was about 30 feet in diameter as a centrepiece. I decided that it would be interesting for the public to walk around the globe, to see the interior, the core of the globe with the magma coming to the surface. It was not that easy because we started with a globe and then we had four globes inside it and the hottest light had to come from the inside without melting everything else. But it worked and the public just loved it.

Cristina Bechtler   What was the theme of the exhibition?

Ken Adam   Science.

Cristina Bechtler   Where has it all gone?

Ken Adam   They were trying to keep it and sell bits of it. I designed a 70-foot high double helix in steel. One has to reduce it and make it smaller and smaller. I found a young

verstand ich nicht recht – es war eine sehr elitäre wissenschaftliche Ausstellung und ich bin absolut nicht … Also griff ich die Idee auf, die Gereon ursprünglich vorgeschwebt hatte. Es gab zwei antike Globen irgendwo in Frankreich, aber sie nach Berlin zu transportieren war ein Problem, also sagte ich: „Lasst mich einen Globus machen!". Ich baute einen von etwa 9 Meter Durchmesser als zentrales Stück. Ich fand, es wäre spannend für die Besucher, um den Globus herumzugehen und das Innere zu sehen, den Kern des Globus mit dem zur Oberfläche aufsteigenden Magma. Es war nicht leicht, weil wir mit einem Globus begannen und am Ende vier Globen in dem einen drin steckten, und das stärkste Licht musste ganz von innen kommen, ohne alles andere zum Schmelzen zu bringen. Aber es funktionierte und das Publikum war begeistert.

Cristina Bechtler   Was war das Thema der Ausstellung?

Ken Adam   Die Naturwissenschaft.

Cristina Bechtler   Und wo ist das Ganze jetzt?

Installation view interior *Theatrum naturae et artis, Wunderkammern des Wissens,* Martin-Gropius-Bau, Berlin, 2000

sculptor in Berlin who was able to make a brilliant reduction of it. It was a very difficult thing to do.

\* \* \*

Bice Curiger   I would like to ask you about the drawings. Do you also use a grey felt pen or only a black one?

Ken Adam   Just black. But I am not allowed to use that ink any longer because its poisonous. It is a translucent ink. It was fantastic for me because I developed a style by controlling the density of my lines. It was unbelievably important because it released me from my inhibitions – coming from a well-to-do upper-middle class German family where my step into art was a painting of a deer. I had an uncle who thought he was an artist and I was so proud of it and showed him the picture and he said, "Es sieht wie Spinat und Ei aus." [It looks like spinach and egg.] That finished me. So I started to do more copying; I was good at it until I managed to release myself. My wife was very much responsible for that too. She is Italian. Born with good taste. I was

Ken Adam   Sie versuchten, es zu erhalten und Teile davon zu verkaufen. Ich entwarf eine 21 Meter hohe Doppelhelix aus Stahl. Man musste sie verkleinern und immer kleiner und kleiner machen. Ich fand einen jungen Bildhauer in Berlin, der in der Lage war, eine brillante Verkleinerung davon anzufertigen. Das war eine extrem schwierige Sache.

\* \* \*

Bice Curiger   Ich habe eine Frage zu den Zeichnungen. Verwenden Sie auch einen grauen Filzstift oder nur einen schwarzen?

Ken Adam   Nur schwarz. Aber ich darf diese Tusche nicht mehr verwenden, weil sie giftig ist. Es ist eine durchscheinende Tusche. Sie war fantastisch für mich, weil ich über die Kontrolle der Strichdichte einen Stil entwickelt habe. Das war unwahrscheinlich wichtig, weil es mich von meinen Hemmungen befreite – ich stamme aus einer gut betuchten deutschen Familie der oberen Mittelschicht und mein erster künstlerischer Gehversuch war das Bild eines Hirsches. Ich hatte einen Onkel, der sich als Künstler betrachtete, und ich zeigte ihm das Bild voller Stolz, und er sagte: „Es sieht wie Spinat und Ei aus." Das machte mich fertig. Also begann ich mehr zu

doing these big sketches 55 years ago. Labouring over every line. She used to take my little scribbles out of the wastepaper basket. There was another famous curator from Berlin, Lotte Eisner. She was the curator of the cinémathèque in Paris and a friend of my mother's. She used to visit when she came to London and she took the scribbles my wife had saved for the cinémathèque. She said, "They're much more alive than these enormous sketches you do." So that felt pen really let me attack my designs, my drawings, released me from my inhibitions.

Hans Ulrich Obrist   What about your drawings, Katharina?

Katharina Fritsch   I don't do drawings.

Bice Curiger   Don't you make any sketches?

Katharina Fritsch   Yes, I have the best ideas in the morning in bed with my coffee, when I have a quiet time. Then I make little sketches, mostly on old envelopes. Afterwards I go to the studio and usually build models with cardboard. Sometimes on a smaller

kopieren; darin war ich gut, bis es mir gelang, davon loszukommen. Meine Frau hat dazu viel beigetragen. Sie ist Italienerin, von Geburt an geschmackssicher. Vor 55 Jahren machte ich diese großen Zeichnungen. Jeder Strich harte Arbeit. Sie fischte jeweils die kleinen Skizzen aus dem Papierkorb. Dann war da noch eine berühmte Dame aus Berlin, Lotte Eisner. Sie war Kuratorin der Cinémathèque française in Paris und eine Freundin meiner Mutter. Auch sie meinte: „Die sind viel lebendiger als diese riesigen Zeichnungen, die du machst." So ermöglichte mir dieser Filzstift, meine Entwürfe, meine Zeichnungen in Angriff zu nehmen, und befreite mich von meinen Hemmungen.

Hans Ulrich Obrist   Wie steht's mit deinen Zeichnungen, Katharina?

Katharina Fritsch   Ich mache keine Zeichnungen.

Bice Curiger   Du machst keine Skizzen?

Katharina Fritsch   Doch, die besten Ideen habe ich am Morgen im Bett beim Kaffee, wenn alles ruhig ist. Dann mache ich kleine Skizzen, meist auf alte Briefumschläge. Danach gehe ich ins

scale, sometimes one-to-one. I do a lot with models because I always have to see it in three dimensions.

Ken Adam   What time do you wake up?

Katharina Fritsch   Very early, six o'clock.

Ken Adam   I go swimming at six a.m. Do you have anxiety?

Katharina Fritsch   No, I just wake up. Not from anxiety. I am very fresh in the morning and very tired in the evening. I have had a strange rhythm for a few years now. Maybe because one gets older. When I was younger, I was more anxious, especially in the early hours, around four or five. That's when I did the piece with the mouse, *Mann und Maus,* where the big mouse sits on the man. It's the time of nightmares, of panic. I read once, or maybe Iwona Blazwick told me, when she was Tate curator, that it's in our genes. It is a kind of archaic reaction, when sleeping before dawn was the most dangerous time.

Atelier und baue gewöhnlich Modelle aus Karton. Manchmal in einem kleineren Maßstab, manchmal 1:1. Ich arbeite viel mit Modellen, weil ich immer alles dreidimensional sehen muss.

Ken Adam   Wann wachen Sie auf?

Katharina Fritsch   Sehr früh, um sechs Uhr.

Ken Adam   Ich gehe um sechs schwimmen. Haben Sie Angstzustände?

Katharina Fritsch   Nein, ich erwache einfach. Nicht aus Angst. Ich bin sehr frisch am Morgen und sehr müde am Abend. Ich habe seit einigen Jahren einen seltsamen Rhythmus. Vielleicht, weil ich älter werde. Als ich noch jünger war, war ich unruhiger, besonders in den frühen Morgenstunden, um vier oder fünf. Damals machte ich die Arbeit mit der Maus, *Mann und Maus,* in der die große Maus auf dem Mann hockt. Das ist die Zeit der Alpträume, der Panik. Ich habe einmal gelesen, oder vielleicht hat es mir Iwona Blazwick erzählt, als sie noch Kuratorin in der Tate Gallery war, dass wir das in den Genen haben: Es ist eine Art archaische Reaktion aus der Zeit, als der Schlaf kurz vor dem Morgengrauen die gefährlichste Zeit war.

Katharina Fritsch, *Mann und Maus* (Man and Mouse), 1991–92

Bice Curiger    This kind of menace is very James Bond. The fear or terror of being threatened with something in bed like …

Katharina Fritsch    … the snakes, the toxic mouse.

Ken Adam    I know about those anxieties because I suffered from them myself. It's that four o'clock in the morning thing. You wake up and you have to prevent yourself from panicking.

Katharina Fritsch    But it's also because of your biography. You went through the war. I know that from my family, the generation that grew up with anxiety and somehow passed it on to their children. Maybe, when you are German, you are kind of paralyzed by history. But it has made us very self-critical and I think that is good, too.

Hans Ulrich Obrist    It is also true of Switzerland. Rem Koolhaas calls it the 'small-country syndrome'. There is a lot of self-criticism.


Bice Curiger    Diese Art Bedrohung erinnert doch sehr an James Bond. Die Angst oder Panik, von etwas im eigenen Bett bedroht zu werden, wie …

Katharina Fritsch    … den Schlangen, der giftigen Maus.

Ken Adam    Ich kenne diese Ängste, weil ich selbst darunter litt. Es ist dieses Vier-Uhr-Früh-Ding. Man erwacht und muss sich beherrschen, nicht in Panik zu verfallen.

Katharina Fritsch    Aber das hängt auch mit Ihrer Biografie zusammen. Sie haben den Krieg erlebt. Ich kenne das aus meiner Familie, der Generation, die mit der Angst groß wurde und sie irgendwie an die Kinder weitergab. Vielleicht ist man als Deutscher irgendwie gelähmt durch die Geschichte. Aber sie hat uns auch sehr selbstkritisch gemacht, und ich denke, das ist gut so.

Hans Ulrich Obrist    Dasselbe gilt für die Schweiz. Rem Koolhaas nennt es das „small-country syndrom". Ein starker Hang zur Selbstkritik.

Ken Adam    Aber die Schweiz hat doch den Wilhelm Tell …

Ken Adam    But Switzerland has William Tell …

Bice Curiger    That's a myth, a fairy tale. In fact, it was invented by a German, Friedrich Schiller.

Ken Adam    Oh really, you disappoint me.

Katharina Fritsch    The Germans are very precise, but the Swiss are even more so. They are 'über-precise'.

Ken Adam    I always have to think of Orson Wells in *The Third Man,* the famous quote about 500 years of democracy and peace in Switzerland and all they came up with was the cuckoo clock.

Bice Curiger    I love that statement though actually the cuckoo clock comes from the Black Forest in Germany.


Bice Curiger    Das ist ein Mythos, ein Märchen. Tatsächlich ist es die Erfindung eines Deutschen, Friedrich Schiller.

Ken Adam    Wirklich? Sie enttäuschen mich.

Katharina Fritsch    Die Deutschen sind sehr genau, aber die Schweizer sogar noch mehr. Sie sind übergenau.

Ken Adam    Ich muss immer an Orson Welles in *Der dritte Mann* denken, das berühmte Zitat über 500 Jahre Demokratie und Frieden in der Schweiz, und alles, was dabei herauskam, war die Kuckucksuhr.

Bice Curiger    Ich liebe diesen Satz, obwohl auch die Kuckucksuhr eigentlich aus Deutschland stammt, aus dem Schwarzwald.

\* \* \*

Bice Curiger  I also wonder about your treatment of surfaces. They are very important in the sense that you eliminate all the details to try and get at the essence. This is also a form of stylization.

Hans Ulrich Obrist  And I think there is a deep and powerful psychological current almost seething under the smooth surfaces that you both sometimes cultivate.

Ken Adam  That sounds very dramatic. Actually, it can sometimes be quite frightening but I like it.

Bice Curiger  Maybe the newer pieces are more erotic, frivolous …

Katharina Fritsch  I was always erotic, isn't the mouse erotic?

Bice Curiger  Sure, with it's tail …

\* \* \*

Bice Curiger  Ich staune auch über Ihre Oberflächengestaltung. Sie ist sehr wichtig, in dem Sinn, dass Sie alle Details weglassen und versuchen, das Wesentliche herauszuarbeiten. Auch das ist eine Form von Stilisierung.

Hans Ulrich Obrist  Und ich glaube, da ist ein tiefer und starker psychologischer Strom, der fast siedend heiß unter diesen glatten Oberflächen fließt, die von euch beiden kultiviert werden.

Ken Adam  Das klingt extrem dramatisch. Tatsächlich, kann es manchmal ziemlich erschreckend sein, aber es gefällt mir.

Bice Curiger  Vielleicht sind die neueren Arbeiten erotischer, frivoler …

Katharina Fritsch  Ich war schon immer erotisch, ist die Maus etwa nicht erotisch?

Bice Curiger  Natürlich, mit ihrem Schwanz …

Ken Adam   What appealed to you about rats?

Katharina Fritsch   I was invited to do a piece at the Dia Center for the Arts in New York. That was at the end of the 80s and everybody wore black; all of New York was black. And when you think of New York and its streets, you think of rats. I was also impressed by the *Batman* movie, which takes place in Gotham City. I liked the Art Deco buildings and their gargoyles. I wanted to do something between rat and dinosaur and discovered the rat king phenomenon. Biologists found some dried out skeletons of rats with their tails all linked up. It's a terrible situation, wanting to go in different directions but unable to move. It's a mysterious phenomenon. I used this image to create the sculpture for New York. The New Yorkers liked it very much. School classes came and did mathematics there: "If the rat is three meters high, how long is the tail?" So it was a kind of sensational piece. I've done other large pieces, like the green *Elephant*. Maybe it's a cinematic effect, too.

Ken Adam   Was hat Sie an den Ratten gereizt?

Katharina Fritsch   Ich wurde eingeladen, eine Arbeit im Dia Center for the Arts in New York zu realisieren. Das war Ende der Achtzigerjahre und alle trugen schwarz; ganz New York war schwarz. Und wenn man an New York und seine Straßen denkt, fallen einem die Ratten ein. Ich war auch beeindruckt vom *Batman*-Film, der in Gotham City spielt. Mir gefielen diese Art-deco-Gebäude mit ihren dämonischen Wasserspeiern. Ich wollte etwas zwischen Ratte und Dinosaurier machen und stieß auf das Phänomen des Rattenkönigs. Biologen haben vertrocknete Rattenskelette gefunden, deren Schwänze ineinander verschlungen waren. Eine schreckliche Situation, in verschiedene Richtungen rennen zu wollen und sich nicht bewegen zu können! Ein rätselhaftes Phänomen. Ich benutzte dieses Bild für die Skulptur in New York. Den New Yorkern gefiel es sehr. Ganze Schulklassen kamen und trieben dort Mathematik: „Wenn die Ratte drei Meter hoch ist, wie lang ist der Schwanz?" Es war eine Art Sensation. Ich habe auch andere große Arbeiten gemacht, etwa der grüne *Elefant*. Vielleicht ist das auch ein filmischer Effekt.

Katharina Fritsch, *Rattenkönig* (Rat-King), 1991–93

Bice Curiger   I do like the way your images trigger emotion or collective memory. We all have pretty much the same feelings or ideas about the image of a rat or the meaning behind the image.

Cristina Bechtler   But a rat is not a rat. How do you represent a 'rat'? There's no fixed formula. So how do you express the uncanniness, the cool, the undercurrent of meaning? I think the two of you have a very similar way of going about it.

Ken Adam   I think Katharina has crueller instincts. First you see a beautiful red heart and the next thing you see is that it's made out of something incongruous, incompatible.

Katharina Fritsch   I have to do it, it's a little bit like voodoo or even a kind of exorcism. I have a lot of fears. I think about a lot of things that could happen to me. So making an image is a way to overcome that, a way to banish the fear.

Ken Adam   The red heart made of teeth is a wonderful contradiction. And you are fascinated by skulls, too.

Bice Curiger   Ich mag die Art, wie deine Bilder Gefühle auslösen oder das kollektive Gedächtnis anzapfen. Wir haben alle mehr oder weniger dieselben Gefühle oder Vorstellungen beim Bild einer Ratte oder von der Bedeutung hinter dem Bild.

Cristina Bechtler   Aber eine Ratte ist keine Ratte. Wie stellt man eine „Ratte" dar? Es gibt kein klares Rezept. Also, wie bringt man das Unheimliche, das Coole, die verborgene Bedeutung zum Ausdruck? Ich glaube, ihr geht auf sehr ähnliche Weise damit um.

Ken Adam   Ich glaube, Katharina hat die grausameren Instinkte. Zuerst sieht man ein schönes rotes Herz und als nächstes erkennt man, dass es aus etwas besteht, was nicht dazu passt, nicht damit vereinbar ist.

Katharina Fritsch   Ich muss das tun, es ist ein bisschen wie Voodoo oder sogar eine Art Exorzismus. Ich habe viele Ängste. Ich denke viel darüber nach, was mir alles zustoßen könnte. Ein Bild zu schaffen, ist eine Möglichkeit, darüber hinwegzukommen, ein Weg, die Angst zu bannen.

Ken Adam   Das rote Herz aus Zähnen ist ein wunderbarer Widerspruch. Und Totenschädel faszinieren dich auch.

Katharina Fritsch, *Herz mit Zähnen* (Heart with Teeth), 1998

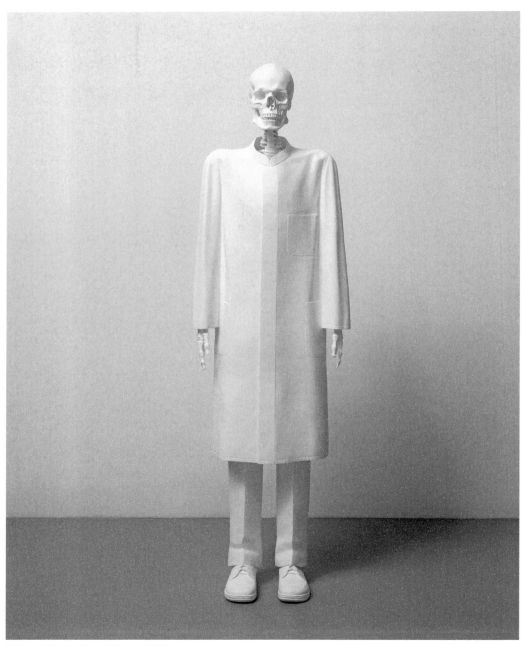

Katharina Fritsch, *Doktor* (Doctor), 1999

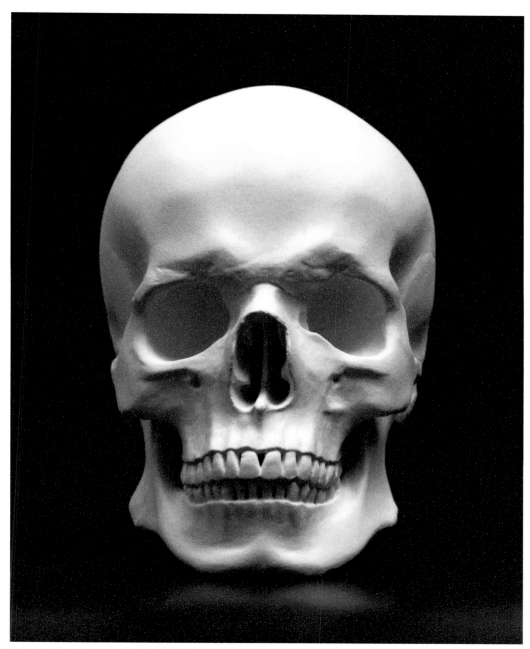

Katharina Fritsch, *Totenkopf* (Skull), 1997/98

Katharina Fritsch   That's something else, a skull is a kind of icon that has always been around in art history. Everybody is fascinated by skulls. I did a figure of a doctor who has a skull as a head.

Ken Adam   It is quite frightening. Like Dr. Mabuse, the villain in Fritz Lang's expressionist films. And the way you made it is brilliant.

Katharina Fritsch   I made a cast so it's very realistic but I wanted to make it so immaterial that it stays as a picture in the mind. That's also related to the movies because they consist of immaterial pictures, created by light. The Public Art Fund in New York asked me to do an outdoor piece for Rockefeller Center. I was going to do a skull with a top hat like Marlene Dietrich. But it was too much black humour for them, too frightening. So I'm working on something else now.

[looking at photographs of her work]


Katharina Fritsch   Das ist etwas anderes, ein Totenkopf ist ein Symbol, das in der Kunstgeschichte immer wieder auftaucht. Jedermann ist fasziniert von Totenschädeln. Ich habe eine Arztfigur gemacht, deren Kopf aus einem Schädel besteht.

Ken Adam   Der ist ziemlich Furcht erregend. Wie Dr. Mabuse, der Bösewicht in Fritz Langs expressionistischen Filmen. Und die Art, wie Sie ihn gemacht haben, ist brillant.

Katharina Fritsch   Ich habe einen Abguss gemacht, er ist also sehr wirklichkeitsgetreu, aber ich wollte, dass er so immateriell wirkt, dass er als Bild im Kopf hängen bleibt. Das hat auch mit dem Film zu tun, weil Filme aus immateriellen Bildern zusammengesetzt sind, die durch Licht entstehen. Der Public Art Fund in New York bat mich, eine Freilichtskulptur für das Rockefeller Center zu schaffen. Ich dachte an einen Totenschädel mit einem Zylinder, wie ihn Marlene Dietrich getragen hat. Aber das war ihnen zu viel schwarzer Humor, zu erschreckend. Also arbeite ich jetzt an etwas anderem.

[Fotografien ihrer Arbeiten anschauend]

Katharina Fritsch, design for a sculpture in front of the Rockefeller Center, New York, 2006

Installation view exhibition Katharina Fritsch,
Museum für Gegenwartskunst Basel, 1997

And these here are brains. I did a multiple. You can buy a brain. I do little sculptures in large, unlimited editions. So whoever wants a brain can buy one from me. I decided to create shelves for goods, something like a department store. I was playing around with the architectural idea of having a store and creating different kinds of shelves for the multiples. They have different shapes. I made a stacked round tower of the Madonnas and a pyramid of the vases.

And this was at the opening of an exhibition in Cologne. I had identical twins – my gallerist's boyfriend and his brother – sitting at a table, dressed in white shirts and black trousers, a living image. And on the table was the plate I made with a picture of two men sitting at a table and on the table a plate with a picture of two men sitting at a table and on the table…

* * *

Und das hier sind Gehirne. Ich habe ein Multiple gemacht. Man kann sich ein Gehirn kaufen. Ich mache kleine Skulpturen in großen, nicht limitierten Editionen. So kann sich jeder, der ein Gehirn will, eines von mir kaufen. Ich beschloss Warenregale zu entwerfen, eine Art Warenhaus. Ich spielte mit der architektonischen Idee, einen Laden zu haben und verschiedene Regale für die Multiples zu entwerfen. Sie haben unterschiedliche Formen. Ich machte einen stapelartigen Turm mit den Madonnen und eine Pyramide mit den Vasen. Und das war bei einer Ausstellungseröffnung in Köln. Da saßen zwei genau gleich aussehende Zwillinge – der Freund meines Galeristen und sein Bruder – in weißem Hemd und schwarzer Hose an einem Tisch, ein lebendes Bild. Und auf dem Tisch lag mein Druckstock eines Bildes von zwei Männern, die an einem Tisch sitzen, auf dem ein Druckstock mit dem Bild von zwei Männern an einem Tisch liegt, und auf dem Tisch …

* * *

Bice Curiger    Ich möchte noch etwas über Bilder reden und die Art, wie ihr mit ihnen umgeht. Die Moderne und die abstrakte Kunst waren das genaue Gegenteil des Bildes. Sie versuchten eine autonome Realität zu schaffen.

Katharina Fritsch, *Warengestell mit Gehirnen* (Display Stand with Brains), 1989

Bice Curiger   I want to talk some more about images and the way you use them. Modernism and abstract art were the exact opposite of the image. They tried to create an autonomous reality.

Katharina Fritsch   When I was at art school, art was very minimal. You couldn't do anything representational. So when I came up with my objects at the Kunstakademie Düsseldorf, it wasn't considered serious art. Then, at the beginning of the 80s, art started getting more extroverted and more colourful. My generation wasn't just focusing on art history but also on movies and American culture. Movies were very important for my generation.

Bice Curiger   Still, I don't think you do specifically American art. Your work might have Pop elements but it's more rigorous and it resonates with an older cultural heritage, older memories. You deal with fairytales, the money is not new money, it is the money of fairytales, the taler. But, of course, there is no conventional narration. In dance theatre, for example, where different disciplines come together, the image acquires meaning it didn't have before – it's as important as the movement. Like what Pina Bausch does or

Katharina Fritsch   Als ich auf die Kunstschule ging, war Kunst gleichbedeutend mit Minimal Art. Man konnte nichts Gegenständliches machen. Als ich an der Kunstakademie Düsseldorf meine Objekte präsentierte, galt das nicht als ernstzunehmende Kunst. Dann, zu Beginn der Achtzigerjahre, begann die Kunst extravertierter und farbiger zu werden. Meine Generation befasste sich nicht nur mit Kunstgeschichte, sondern auch mit Filmen und mit der amerikanischen Kultur. Filme waren für meine Generation sehr wichtig.

Bice Curiger   Trotzdem, ich denke nicht, dass du spezifisch amerikanische Kunst machst. Deine Arbeit mag Pop-Elemente aufweisen, aber sie ist strenger und es schwingt ein älteres kulturelles Erbe in ihr mit, ältere Erinnerungen. Du setzt dich mit Märchen auseinander, das Geld ist kein neues Geld, es ist auch das Geld der Märchen, der Taler. Aber es gibt natürlich keine konventionelle Erzählform. Im Tanztheater, zum Beispiel, wo verschiedene Disziplinen zusammenfließen, bekommt das Bild eine Bedeutung, die es früher nicht hatte – es ist gleich wichtig wie die Bewegung. Etwa bei Pina Bausch oder bei Regisseuren wie Christoph Marthaler und Robert Wilson –, während es bei dir diese Linearität der Entwicklung oder Erzählung nicht mehr gibt.

Ken Adam, drawing of the interior of the vast Polka Saloon, Act I, *La Fanciulla del West,* Covent Garden production, London, 1977

stage directors like Christoph Marthaler and Robert Wilson – where you don't have this linearity of development or narration anymore.

Hans Ulrich Obrist    Ken, haven't you recently been working on an opera?

Ken Adam    Covent Garden has revived the Puccini opera *La Fanciulla del West* with reconstructions of the sets I designed thirty years ago. It's a successful opera but very dependent on the soprano, the tenor and the orchestra. I did the opera again in Spoleto in Italy and in America. They revive it from time to time and I suddenly find myself in a completely different world. The Italian director Piero Faggioni is the same one who was with me when we first did it at Covent Garden 31 years ago. Zubin Mehta, a Hollywood conductor, had lunch with somebody called Lew Wasserman, who was a big chief at Universal Studios and a supervising art director. I'm talking about thirty years ago. They wanted to revive *La Fanciulla*, which was first performed in New York with Caruso singing the male tenor part. They decided it needed a film designer because it had to be real. That's why they contacted me. I knew nothing about opera. There is a little bit of expressionism in

Hans Ulrich Obrist    Ken, haben Sie nicht kürzlich an einer Oper mitgewirkt?

Ken Adam    Covent Garden hat Puccinis Oper *La Fanciulla del West* wiederaufgeführt, mit Nachbauten des Bühnenbildes, das ich vor 30 Jahren entworfen habe. Es ist eine erfolgreiche Oper, die jedoch mit dem Sopran, dem Tenor und dem Orchester steht und fällt. Ich habe diese Oper auch noch in Spoleto, Italien, und in Amerika gemacht. Sie holen sie von Zeit zu Zeit aus der Versenkung und ich finde mich in einer völlig anderen Welt wieder. Der italienische Regisseur Piero Faggioni ist derselbe, mit dem ich beim ersten Mal, vor 31 Jahren, am Covent Garden zusammengearbeitet habe. Zubin Mehta, der damals in Hollywood dirigierte, sprach beim Lunch mit jemandem namens Lew Wasserman, ein großer Boss bei Universal Studios und ein leitender Art Director. Das war vor 30 Jahren. Sie wollten *La Fanciulla* wiederbeleben, die in New York mit Caruso als Tenor uraufgeführt worden war. Sie fanden, dazu bräuchten sie einen Filmdesigner, weil es realistisch wirken musste. Deshalb haben sie mich kontaktiert. Ich hatte keine Ahnung von Oper. Das Bühnenbild hat einen ganz leicht expressionistischen Zug, aber insgesamt ist es sehr naturalistisch. Ich würde so etwas heute nicht mehr machen, aber damals war es interessant. Und sie holen es immer wieder hervor.

Ken Adam, drawing of the Mining Camp, Act III, *La Fanciulla del West*, Covent Garden production, London, 1977

the set but on the whole it's very naturalistic. I would never do anything like that today but it was interesting at the time. And they keep reviving it.

Bice Curiger  Katharina, what is the most realistic thing you've done if you think in those terms?

Katharina Fritsch  Maybe the human figures.

Hans Ulrich Obrist  Or the *Elephant*.

Katharina Fritsch  The *Elephant* (1987), yes. The directors of the Kaiser Wilhelm Museum in Krefeld asked me if I could do a piece in a room that looked to me like a winter garden from the 19th century. I immediately had this vision of an elephant, like a big plant. When I told the directors, they just laughed because they only had 12,000 DM for the whole show, including the catalogue. They gave me 6,000 DM. It was my first big museum piece. The Museum of Natural History gave me the forms and I made a cast

Bice Curiger  Katharina, was ist, vor diesem Hintergrund betrachtet, das Realistischste, was du je gemacht hast?

Katharina Fritsch  Vielleicht die menschlichen Figuren.

Hans Ulrich Obrist  Oder der *Elefant*.

Katharina Fritsch  Der *Elefant* (1987), ja. Die Direktoren des Kaiser Wilhelm Museums in Krefeld fragten mich, ob ich eine Arbeit für einen Raum schaffen könnte, der für mich wie ein Wintergarten aus dem 19. Jahrhundert aussah. Ich hatte sofort die Vision von einem Elefanten, wie eine große Pflanze. Als ich das den Direktoren mitteilte, lachten sie nur, weil sie gerade mal 12.000 DM für die ganze Ausstellung zur Verfügung hatten, den Katalog mit eingeschlossen. Sie gaben mir 6.000 DM. Das war mein erstes großes Werk für ein Museum. Das naturhistorische Museum stellte mir die Gussformen zur Verfügung und ich machte einen Abguss des Elefanten, veränderte aber den Rüssel ein wenig. Er ist lebensgroß, grün bemalt und steht auf einem Podest.

of the elephant but I changed the trunk a little bit. It's life size, painted green and on a pedestal.

Ken Adam    That's fantastic. So did you build a scaffold?

Katharina Fritsch    First we got the forms from the Museum König in Bonn and transported them to Krefeld. I went there by tram every day. Only one person helped me, I was totally driven, I had to do it. The museum built the oval pedestal. The whole thing is about 14 feet high. In a way, it was a kind of film scene in a museum, otherwise filled with minimal art. I liked the idea of visitors being very sophisticated about Donald Judd and all the minimal art and then turning the corner and … The first thing you saw through the door was the trunk, and then all of a sudden there was this big green elephant. Some of my colleagues, like Thomas Schütte or Harald Klingelhöller, were very intellectual and minimal. I wanted to joke a little bit about that.

Hans Ulrich Obrist    So was it a reaction to something?


Ken Adam    Fantastisch. Dann haben Sie ein Gerüst gebaut?

Katharina Fritsch    Zuerst haben wir die Formen vom Museum König in Bonn bekommen und sie nach Krefeld transportiert. Ich fuhr jeden Tag mit der Trambahn hin. Nur eine einzige Person half mir dabei, ich war total besessen, ich musste es einfach tun. Das Museum baute das ovale Podest. Das Ganze ist gut 4 Meter hoch. In gewisser Weise war es eine Filmszene in einem Museum, das sonst voller Minimal Art war. Mir gefiel die Vorstellung, dass Besucher, die sich gewählt über Donald Judd und die ganze Minimal Art ausließen, um die Ecke biegen würden und … Das erste, was man durch die Tür erblickte, war der Rüssel, und dann stand da plötzlich dieser große grüne Elefant. Einige meiner Kollegen, wie Thomas Schütte oder Harald Klingelhöller, gaben sich sehr intellektuell, an Minimal Art und am postmodernen Diskurs orientiert. Ich wollte darüber etwas witzeln.

Hans Ulrich Obrist    Dann war es eine Reaktion auf etwas?

Katharina Fritsch    Nicht wirklich. Es ist nicht gut, zu reagieren. Es war eher wie ein Nebeneffekt. Ich glaubte an das Bild, und irgendwie war es auch eine Aussage – man würde in einem Museum nie einen grünen Elefanten erwarten. Es war etwas Neues.

Katharina Fritsch, *Elefant* (Elephant), 1987

Katharina Fritsch   Not really. It is not good to react. It was more like a side effect. I believed in the image and, in way, it was a statement – you would never expect to find a green elephant in a museum. So it was something new.

Ken Adam   What material did you use?

Katharina Fritsch   Polyester with fibber glass inside.

Ken Adam   The scale is unbelievable. A gigantic task.

Katharina Fritsch   A lot of my pieces are big, like the *Rat King*. It is huge, about 43 feet in diameter. You can see it at the Schaulager in Basel. I think I was always inspired by Hollywood. It could be in an exotic movie, the queen of darkness…

Hans Ulrich Obrist   Katharina has told us about her *Brain*. Can you tell us about your brain, Ken?


Ken Adam   Welches Material haben Sie verwendet?

Katharina Fritsch   Polyester verstärkt mit Fiberglasfasern.

Ken Adam   Die Größe ist unglaublich. Eine gigantische Aufgabe.

Katharina Fritsch   Viele meiner Arbeiten sind groß, auch der *Rattenkönig*. Er ist riesig, etwa 13 Meter im Durchmesser. Man kann ihn im Schaulager Basel anschauen. Ich glaube, ich war schon immer von Hollywood inspiriert. Die Szene könnte aus einem exotischen Film sein, die Königin der Dunkelheit …

Hans Ulrich Obrist   Katharina hat uns von ihrem *Gehirn* erzählt. Was können Sie uns über Ihr Gehirn verraten, Ken?

Ken Adam   Das war eine Idee für den Film *Star Trek*. Doch die Dreharbeiten wurden um eineinhalb Jahre verschoben. Phil Kaufmann sollte Regie führen. Über eine Zivilisation 2000 Jahre in der

Ken Adam, concept drawing of the Meditation Chamber for *Star Trek,* 1977

Ken Adam, study for The Super Brain for *Star Trek*, 1977

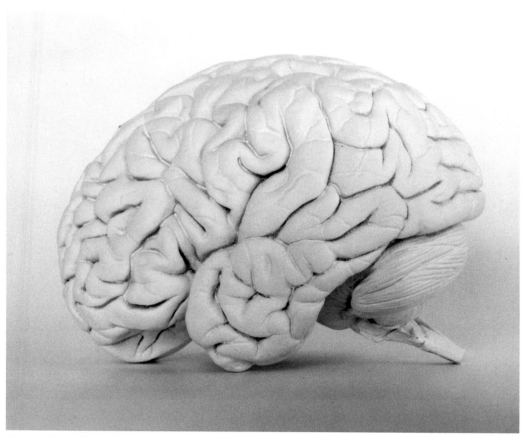

Katharina Fritsch, *Gehirn* (Brain), 1987/89

Ken Adam    It was an idea for *Star Trek*. We were going to make the film but it was postponed for a year and a half. Phil Kaufmann was going to direct it. About a civilization 2000 years from now. I came up with this super brain and I liked it actually. But it never came about.

\* \* \*

Cristina Bechtler    You both use the "spider" and the "fly" in your work.

Ken Adam    When I look at your sculpture of a fly, I can see what you are interested in. I mean, it could also be a model aircraft.

Katharina Fritsch    Yes, it is very technical. I like the idea that you use a marker. It's a technical instrument, too. You avoid emotions in your drawing, so the emotion comes from the light and not from your treatment of line. I can appreciate that. I also like to work with machines. I have fallen in love with 3D prints. You can scan things and then print a three-dimensional version.

Zukunft. Ich hatte diese Idee mit dem Superhirn und mochte sie wirklich. Doch dann ist es nie dazu gekommen.

\*\*\*

Cristina Bechtler    Ihr verwendet beide sowohl „die Spinne" wie „die Fliege" in euren Arbeiten.

Ken Adam    Wenn ich Ihre Skulptur einer Fliege anschaue, sehe ich sofort, was Sie daran interessiert. Ich meine, es könnte auch ein Modellflugzeug sein.

Katharina Fritsch    Ja, sie ist sehr technisch. Mir gefällt die Vorstellung, dass Sie mit einem Filzstift arbeiten. Das ist auch ein technisches Instrument. Sie vermeiden Emotionen in Ihren Zeichnungen, so entsteht die Emotion durch das Licht und nicht durch die Art Ihrer Linienführung. Das kann ich nachvollziehen. Ich arbeite auch gerne mit Maschinen. Ich bin ganz verliebt in 3D-Prints. Man kann Dinge scannen und dann dreidimensionale Ansichten ausdrucken.

Ken Adam    Sie sind viel moderner als ich, ich habe nicht einmal einen Computer.

Ken Adam   You are much more modern than I am because I haven't got a computer.

Katharina Fritsch   It is a relatively new technique and I use it sometimes to make the figures. We used to make models and then forms to cast them in. Now I can just scan the things or figures of the people and then rework them in 3D. The way figures are constructed on a computer could be something out of a James Bond film.

Cristina Bechtler   Q was your idea?

Ken Adam   Yes, the gadget man.

Katharina Fritsch   I love Q, his inventions – the clock with the saw in it. Or the pen you can shoot with. And Bond always ends up in situations where he can use these things.

Ken Adam   It was not always my idea. I had a very good team of people around me, particularly for the special effects.


Katharina Fritsch   Es ist eine relativ neue Technik und ich verwende sie manchmal, um Figuren zu erarbeiten. Früher haben wir Modelle gemacht und dann Gussformen, um sie abzugießen. Jetzt kann ich Dinge oder menschliche Figuren einfach scannen und dann in 3D überarbeiten. Die Art, wie Figuren auf dem Computer konstruiert werden, könnte aus einem James-Bond-Film stammen.

Cristina Bechtler   War Q Ihre Idee?

Ken Adam   Ja, der Mann fürs technische Spielzeug.

Katharina Fritsch   Ich liebe Q, seine Erfindungen – die Uhr mit eingebauter Säge oder den Kugelschreiber, mit dem man schießen kann. Und Bond gerät immer in Situationen, in denen er diese Dinge gebrauchen kann.

Ken Adam   Das waren nicht immer meine Ideen. Ich hatte ein sehr gutes Team von Leuten um mich herum, besonders für die Spezialeffekte.

Katharina Fritsch, *Fliege* (Fly), 2000

Katharina Fritsch    It must have been a lot of fun to do all that designing.

Ken Adam    Particularly for me because I was a sports car fiend. I had an E-Type Jaguar and every time I came out somebody had banged into it, so I got my own back. Q was really born in *Goldfinger*, because for *Dr. No* we had no gadgets. I didn't do *From Russia With Love,* where they had Lotte Lenya with the spike in her shoe. But on *Goldfinger* we really started with that kind of thing, the Aston Martin. *Thunderball* was a different dimension because everything was underwater. We trained for two or three weeks in a swimming pool and then we all went underwater, which was not so pleasant because there were sharks around. What was almost more dangerous were those weapons under water. The underwater director Ricou Browning, who directed the *Flipper* series (1964) in Florida, was struck by an arrow straight through his thigh. They are very powerful weapons, even under water. There are a lot of anecdotes but that would be out of context and I don't want to frighten you.

Katharina Fritsch    No, no, it's very interesting.

Katharina Fritsch    Das muss ein Riesenspaß gewesen sein, all diese Dinge zu gestalten.

Ken Adam    Besonders für mich, weil ich von Sportwagen besessen war. Ich hatte einen Jaguar E-Type und jedes Mal, wenn ich raus kam, hatte jemand nicht aufgepasst und eine Beule oder einen Kratzer gemacht, also habe ich mich dafür gerächt. Q wurde für *Goldfinger* erfunden, denn in *Dr. No* hatten wir kein technisches Spielzeug. *From Russia With Love* habe ich nicht gemacht, dort hatten sie Lotte Lenya mit dem Stachel im Schuh. Aber bei *Goldfinger* begannen wir so richtig mit diesen Dingen, dem Aston Martin. *Thunderball* war eine andere Dimension, weil alles unter Wasser spielte, was nicht so lustig war, denn es schwammen überall Haie herum. Was aber fast noch gefährlicher war, waren all diese Waffen unter Wasser. Der Regisseur für die Unterwasserszenen, Ricou Browning, der die *Flipper*-Serie (1964) in Florida gemacht hatte, wurde von einem Pfeil voll in die Hüfte getroffen. Das sind sehr starke Waffen, selbst unter Wasser. Dazu gibt's eine Menge Anekdoten, aber das würde den Rahmen hier sprengen und ich möchte Sie nicht erschrecken.

Katharina Fritsch    Nein, nein, das ist doch sehr spannend.

Ken Adam, sketches of the Aston Martin DB5 for *Goldfinger*, 1964

Ken Adam   The next thing you do will be a gigantic shark!

Katharina Fritsch   I wanted to do a shark once…

Bice Curiger   But then Damien Hirst stole the idea.

Katharina Fritsch   He made his shark a few years later, but mine would have been more elegant. I will make it one day.

Hans Ulrich Obrist   Can you tell us more about your unrealized project?

Katharina Fritsch   I made a model for the show in Basel. I still have it but then I did *Company at Table* instead. I had planned to do a kind of horror scenario – a ghost with a pool of blood and a shark in a plexiglass cube. It was going to be three meters long and on a chrome construction – a minimal piece with a shark inside. I wanted it to look frozen, like in a paperweight. Doing the shark would have been expensive and it was difficult to put it in plexiglass without bubbles, so it never came about, but everybody

Ken Adam   Das nächste, was Sie machen, wird ein gigantischer Hai sein!

Katharina Fritsch   Tatsächlich wollte ich einmal einen Hai machen

Bice Curiger   Aber dann hat Damien Hirst die Idee gestohlen.

Katharina Fritsch   Er hat seinen Hai ein paar Jahre später gebracht, aber meiner wäre eleganter gewesen. Eines Tages werde ich ihn machen.

Hans Ulrich Obrist   Kannst du uns etwas mehr über dieses nicht realisierte Projekt erzählen?

Katharina Fritsch   Ich habe ein Modell für die Ausstellung in Basel gemacht. Ich habe es immer noch, aber dann realisierte ich stattdessen die *Tischgesellschaft*. Ich hatte eine Art Horrorszenario geplant – ein Geist mit einer Blutlache und ein Hai in einem Plexiglasrechteck. Es sollte drei Meter lang werden und einen Chromstahlsockel haben – ein Minimal-Kunstwerk mit einem Hai drin. Er sollte wie erstarrt wirken, wie in einem gläsernen Briefbeschwerer. Die

was talking about it and three years later Damien Hirst popped up with it and got famous.

Ken Adam   But in formaldehyde.

Katharina Fritsch   I think my sculpture would have been more abstract. It would have been a cast and therefore hopefully lighter and more elegant.

Hans Ulrich Obrist   It could still be realized.

Katharina Fritsch   Yes, I'm thinking about how to resolve the technical issues.

Ken Adam   You are pretty busy.

Katharina Fritsch   It is so nice that somebody says that.


Produktion des Hais wäre teuer geworden und es war schwierig, ihn in Plexiglas einzuschließen, ohne dass Luftblasen entstanden; so kam es nie dazu, aber alle sprachen darüber, und drei Jahre später tauchte plötzlich Damien Hirst damit auf und wurde berühmt.

Ken Adam   Aber in Formaldehyd.

Katharina Fritsch   Ich glaube, meine Skulptur wäre abstrakter geworden. Es wäre ein Abguss gewesen und deshalb hoffentlich leichter und eleganter.

Hans Ulrich Obrist   Es ließe sich immer noch realisieren.

Katharina Fritsch   Ja, ich denke darüber nach, wie man das technisch lösen könnte.

Ken Adam   Sie sind ziemlich fleißig.

Katharina Fritsch   Es ist so schön, dass jemand das sagt.

Katharina Fritsch, *Hai* (Shark), model, 1987/2007

Bice Curiger   You mentioned 'elegance'. The idea of elegance is important in your work.

Ken Adam   I never thought of that but you are probably right.

Katharina Fritsch   The Bond world is very elegant, too – and very light. There's nothing heavy about it.

Bice Curiger   It's a question of form. Everything fits, it's all of a piece, rounded out – the shape of the pool and even the shape of nature.

Katharina Fritsch   When you use the word 'elegant' in art, you always have a problem. Hardliners are very negative when it's applied to sculpture. But I think elegance also means that something is lighter. Sculptures are heavier, heavy metal. I hate things that are heavy. This is something we might have in common, too.

Ken Adam   I am fascinated. Actually, I wasn't all that aware of your computer-aided model-making and sculpture.

Bice Curiger   Du hast von Eleganz gesprochen. Die Idee der Eleganz ist für euch beide wichtig.

Ken Adam   Daran habe ich gar nie gedacht, aber wahrscheinlich haben Sie recht.

Katharina Fritsch   Die Bond-Welt ist sehr elegant – und sehr leicht. Da gibt es nichts, was schwer wirkt.

Bice Curiger   Das ist alles eine Frage der Form. Alles passt, das Ganze ist aus einem Guss, abgerundet – die Form des Swimmingpools und sogar die Natur.

Katharina Fritsch   Wenn man in der Kunst das Wort „elegant" verwendet, hat man immer ein Problem. Puristen reagieren sehr ablehnend, wenn man das von einer Skulptur sagt. Aber ich glaube, Eleganz bedeutet auch, dass etwas leichter wirkt. Skulpturen sind eher schwer, aus schwerem Metall. Ich hasse alles Schwere. Das verbindet uns vielleicht auch.

Ken Adam   Ich bin fasziniert. Mir war überhaupt nicht bewusst, dass Sie Modelle und Skulpturen mithilfe des Computers erarbeiten.

Katharina Fritsch    I'm not so good at it. I might start at the computer and tell my assistant to make it this colour or that, but then I go to the studio and make a cardboard model. Deciding things on the computer is difficult because you don't have the third dimension.

Ken Adam    When you see computer designed architecture, you immediately recognize it.

Hans Ulrich Obrist    Interestingly enough, even though you don't use the computer, you did design a computer game in 2003, *Goldeneye: Rogue Agent.* And there is also a scene of Switzerland in it.

Ken Adam    It was cut out of the game. I was in England; the developers Electronic Arts were in Hollywood. The next thing I knew was that Switzerland had been eliminated. Not all of it but a lot of it. I didn't use a computer; I did my sketches in the usual way and had a young assistant who emailed them to Electronic Arts. Eventually I went over there and I practically had a heart attack when I saw what they did with my designs. In the computer game everything has to work and you have to allow for spaces where

Katharina Fritsch    Ich bin gar nicht so gut darin. Ich beginne vielleicht am Computer und weise meinen Assistenten an, es mit dieser oder jener Farbe zu versuchen, aber dann gehe ich in mein Atelier und baue ein Kartonmodell. Es ist schwierig, Dinge am Computer zu entscheiden, weil die dritte Dimension fehlt.

Ken Adam    Bei Architektur, die mit Computer Aided Design entworfen wurde, sieht man das sofort.

Hans Ulrich Obrist    Obwohl Sie nicht mit dem Computer arbeiten, haben Sie im Jahr 2003 interessanterweise ein Computerspiel gestaltet, *Goldeneye: Rogue Agent.* Und darin gibt es auch eine Szene, die in der Schweiz spielt.

Ken Adam    Die wurde aus dem Spiel herausgeschnitten. Ich saß in England; die Entwickler, Electronic Arts, saßen in Hollywood. Und plötzlich hörte ich, dass die Schweiz herausgenommen worden war. Nicht alles, aber ein großer Teil davon. Ich habe nicht mit dem Computer gearbeitet; ich habe meine Zeichnungen gemacht wie üblich und hatte einen jungen Assistenten, der sie per E-Mail an Electronic Arts sandte. Schließlich flog ich einmal hinüber

the characters can hide or shoot from. That was new to me. But I think they learned more from me than I did from them.

Hans Ulrich Obrist    One character, who seems to be an Ex-British agent, has defected to the other side and works for both *Dr. No* and *Goldfinger*. He's in between, he has a cybernetic eye. Wasn't that your idea?

Ken Adam    No, that was in the script. But you know, there I was working with the biggest computer game company in the world, and they wanted me to redesign the interior of Fort Knox. I thought of adding all sorts of rooms and keeping the main cathedral-like, prison-like room. Then they sent me the DVDs to look at and I couldn't find the gold. I found big crates, in which you could occasionally see a bit of gold. I went crazy. The whole idea of Fort Knox is the gold. They just didn't know how to simulate gold on the computer yet.

Katharina Fritsch    But now they can do hair.


und mich traf fast der Schlag, als ich sah, was sie mit meinen Entwürfen anstellten. In einem Computerspiel ist alles funktional und man muss Orte einplanen, wo die Figuren in Deckung gehen können oder von wo aus sie schießen können. Das war neu für mich. Aber ich glaube, sie haben mehr von mir gelernt als ich von ihnen.

Hans Ulrich Obrist    Eine der Figuren, es scheint ein ehemaliger britischer Agent zu sein, ist zur anderen Seite übergelaufen und arbeitet sowohl für *Dr. No* wie für *Goldfinger*. Er steht dazwischen, er hat ein kybernetisches Auge. War das nicht Ihre Idee?

Ken Adam    Nein, das stand im Drehbuch. Aber wissen Sie, da arbeitete ich nun mit der größten Computerspielfirma auf der Welt, und sie wollten, dass ich das Innere von Fort Knox neu gestalte. Ich dachte daran, allerlei Räume hinzuzufügen und den zentralen Raum beizubehalten, der an eine Kathedrale oder ein Gefängnis erinnert. Dann sandten sie mir die DVDs zum Anschauen und ich konnte kein Gold darin entdecken. Ich sah große Kisten, in denen manchmal ein bisschen Gold aufblitzte. Es war zum Verrücktwerden. Die ganze Idee von Fort Knox ist das Gold. Sie wussten einfach noch nicht, wie man Gold am Computer simulieren kann.

Katharina Fritsch    Aber jetzt können sie Haare darstellen.

Ken Adam   The skin tones are fantastic.

Katharina Fritsch   They can also animate hair and fur. Just look at the mammoths in *Ice Age*.

Ken Adam   It's getting better every day. Almost frightening. But when they produced the game, they couldn't handle reflective surfaces yet. They were going through all the teething problems. None of the people I worked with at Electronic Arts are still with them, they went to Disney or somewhere. There are no unions, so sometimes they work day and night. I didn't like that. It reminded me of the early days in the movies.

Katharina Fritsch   Incidentally, when people talk about the Bond films, they usually think of the early ones. There are so many of them now and they're getting more and more technical and overblown.

Ken Adam   The exciting thing was to try and make them as real as possible, so that the audience knew they weren't being cheated. We did very little cheating. It was quite

Ken Adam   Die Hauttöne sind fantastisch.

Katharina Fritsch   Sie können die Haare und den Pelz auch animieren. Man braucht sich bloß die Mammuts in *Ice Age* anzuschauen.

Ken Adam   Es wird von Tag zu Tag besser. Fast erschreckend. Aber als sie das Spiel produzierten, konnten sie noch nicht mit spiegelnden Oberflächen umgehen. Sie haben noch alle Kinderkrankheiten durchgemacht. Keiner der Leute, die damals bei Electronic Arts arbeiteten, ist heute noch dort, sie gingen alle zu Disney oder anderswohin. Es gibt keine Gewerkschaften, also arbeiteten sie manchmal Tag und Nacht. Das gefiel mir nicht. Es erinnerte mich an die Frühzeit des Films.

Katharina Fritsch   Apropos Frühzeit, wenn die Leute von Bond-Filmen sprechen, denken sie meist an die frühen Filme. Mittlerweile gibt es so viele und sie werden immer technischer und aufgeblähter.

Ken Adam   Das Aufregende daran war damals, alles so realistisch wie möglich zu machen, so dass das Publikum wusste, dass es nicht hinters Licht geführt wurde. Wir schummelten selten.

dangerous at times. I remember the jet pack in *Thunderball*, when he takes off at that chateau. We had an American ex-colonel who used to check out the latest inventions and he found out about this jet pack. It flew for maybe half a minute. He had to fly by a stop watch. But it was real, even though Sean never used it. There was a lot of excitement in that.

Think of special effects pictures like *2001: A Space Odyssey*. I had introduced Stanley to my special effects man Wally Veevers, who was with me for quite some time. He was then in his late sixties, early seventies. He was brilliant. Every time I was in trouble I used to call Wally and he would say, "Don't worry, let me see to it. I'll come up with a solution tomorrow." So in *2001*, eighty per cent of the special effects were done by Wally with worm gears and mechanical devices; the rest, the psychedelic trip, was done by Douglas Trumbull. It was exciting.

Before CGI, directors had to use all their artistic talent and imagination to come up with something that was good – maybe not 200,000 people attacking the walls of Jerusalem …

What was even more important, all the great actors I worked with – Lawrence Olivier, Noël Coward, John Gielgud, Marlon Brando – insisted on the set and the props. It

Das war manchmal ziemlich gefährlich. Ich denke etwa an das Jet-Pack in *Thunderball*, diesen Rucksack mit Düsenantrieb, mit dem Bond vom Schloss wegfliegt. Wir hatten einen ehemaligen Oberst der amerikanischen Armee, der jeweils auf der Jagd nach den neusten Erfindungen war und der stieß auf dieses Jet-Pack. Es flog etwa eine halbe Minute lang. Man musste mit der Stoppuhr fliegen. Aber es war real, auch wenn Sean selbst es nie benutzt hat. Das war mit einiger Aufregung verbunden. Oder denken Sie an Filme mit Spezialeffekten, wie *2001: A Space Odyssey*. Ich hatte Stanley meinen Mann für Spezialeffekte, Wally Veevers, vorgestellt, der ziemlich lange mit mir zusammengearbeitet hat. Er war damals Ende sechzig, Anfang siebzig. Er war brillant. Jedes Mal, wenn ich in Schwierigkeiten war, rief ich Wally an und der sagte: „Mach dir keine Sorgen, ich schau mir das an, morgen habe ich eine Lösung." In 2001 hat Wally 80 Prozent der Spezialeffekte mit Schneckengetrieben und anderen mechanischen Mitteln produziert; den Rest, den psychedelischen Trip, hat Douglas Trumbull gemacht. Es war hoch interessant.

Als es die heutige Computergrafik noch nicht gab, mussten die Regisseure ihr ganzes künstlerisches Talent und ihre Fantasie aufbieten, um gute Lösungen zu finden – nicht unbedingt 200.000 Leute, die die Stadtmauern von Jerusalem stürmen   Und was vielleicht noch wichtiger war, all die großen Schauspieler, mit denen ich zusammengearbeitet habe – Lawrence Olivier, Noël Coward, John Gielgud, Marlon Brando – legten großen Wert auf Bühnenbild und

was part of their trade. Now they have a green or blue screen and nothing else. It is a completely different technique. That's why I like your work; I can appreciate the craft it takes to make it.

Katharina Fritsch    When so much intensity is involved in making something, it gives off a special kind of energy and you can sense that when you look at it. I think there is a kind of truth in that.

Bice Curiger    Yes, when Ken was talking about *Dr. No,* he mentioned trying out every material he could get his hands on. A lot of architecture nowadays tends to use materials in unconventional, unexpected ways so that they look more precious, for instance. The work of Herzog & de Meuron is all about transforming and reinventing materials. Their work has an elegance and a luxury without falling into the trap of the hackneyed vocabulary used, say, in hotel chains.
On a totally different level, we see younger artists, who don't use video but 16 or 8 mm projectors with complicated loop devices.


Requisiten. Das war ein integraler Bestandteil ihres Berufs. Heute hat man nur noch einen Green- oder Bluescreen und sonst nichts. Es ist eine völlig andere Technik. Deshalb gefällt mir Ihre Arbeit; ich weiß um das Handwerk und Können, das dahinter steckt.

Katharina Fritsch    Wenn die Umsetzung von etwas mit so viel Intensität verbunden ist, strahlt es eine besondere Art von Energie aus, die beim Betrachten spürbar ist. Ich glaube, darin zeigt sich eine Art Wahrheit.

Bice Curiger    Ja, als Ken über *Dr. No* sprach, redete er davon, dass er jedes Material ausprobierte, das er in die Hände bekommen konnte. In der Architektur werden heute oft Materialien auf unkonventionelle, überraschende Art eingesetzt, so dass sie beispielsweise kostbarer wirken. In den Arbeiten von Herzog & de Meuron geht es immer auch um das Verwandeln und Neuerfinden von Materialien. Ihre Bauten sind elegant und luxuriös, ohne in die Falle des abgedroschenen Vokabulars zu tappen, das beispielsweise bei Hotelketten zum Einsatz kommt. Auf einer ganz anderen Ebene sehen wir jüngere Künstler, die nicht mit Video arbeiten, sondern mit 16- oder 18-mm-Filmprojektoren mit komplizierter Loop-Technik.

Ken Adam, design concept for the boardroom interior of SPECTRE's headquaters for *Thunderball*, 1965

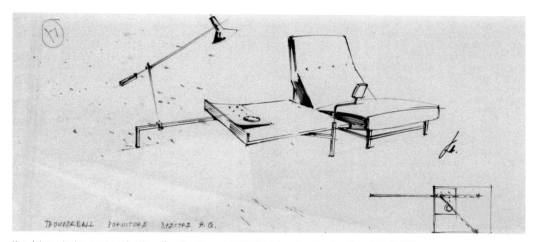

Ken Adam, design concept for the office furniture of SPECTRE's headquaters for *Thunderball*, 1965

Ken Adam, drawing of Largo's Disco Volante yacht for *Thunderball*, 1965

Katharina Fritsch   They are using the old material.

Bice Curiger   I wonder why. Is it the atmosphere, the warmth of the medium? Or is it because they know that actual single images are being projected? Of course, it does put more emphasis on the medium.

Katharina Fritsch   That's like digital vs. analog photography. Digital is brilliant but there is something different about the old material; it has more depth.

Hans Ulrich Obrist   And the importance of drawing. A lot of students have started drawing again. It's a reaction to the disappearance of drawing in the computer age.

Katharina Fritsch   A very strong reaction. I teach at the Kunstakademie in Münster and a lot of my students are really brilliant at making something with their hands. They want that. They want to get back to manual techniques. It's almost as if they had been deprived whereas my generation wanted nothing to do with those traditional skills. In my studio I work with five people and they are all very happy to do hands-on work.

Katharina Fritsch   Sie verwenden das alte Material.

Bice Curiger   Aber warum? Ist es die Atmosphäre, die menschliche Wärme des Mediums? Oder ist es, weil sie wissen, dass dabei eigentlich einzelne Bilder projiziert werden? Natürlich bekommt dadurch das Medium selbst mehr Gewicht.

Katharina Fritsch   Das ist wie digitale versus analoge Fotografie. Digital ist brillant, aber das alte Material ist irgendwie anders; es hat mehr Tiefe.

Hans Ulrich Obrist   Und die Bedeutung der Zeichnung. Viele Studierende haben wieder zu zeichnen begonnen. Es ist eine Reaktion auf das Verschwinden der Zeichnung im Computerzeitalter.

Katharina Fritsch   Eine sehr vehemente Reaktion. Ich unterrichte an der Kunstakademie in Münster und viele Studierende sind richtig gut, sobald es darum geht, etwas mit den eigenen Händen zu machen. Sie wollen das. Sie wollen zurück zu den manuellen Techniken. Es ist fast, als wäre ihnen etwas vorenthalten worden, während meine Generation nichts mehr mit diesen traditionellen Techniken zu tun haben wollte. In meinem Atelier arbeite ich mit fünf Leuten zusammen und sie sind alle ganz glücklich, wenn sie konkret Hand anlegen können.

Ken Adam   I couldn't believe it when I was invited to Norman Foster's firm last year. There were 600 architects all sitting at the computer. There wasn't a single drawing board.

Katharina Fritsch   Sometimes I work at the computer for days and although I'm worn out, I feel as if I haven't done any real work. Maybe it's psychological. It's obviously a useful device and fascinating when I do my three-dimensional prints. It certainly is interesting to be able to scan an existing sculpture and play around with it.

Bice Curiger   In the James Bond films, you have volcanoes, caves, raw nature and stones that are millions of years old and then the other extreme of inconceivably advanced technology, so advanced that it's threatening. Technology, nature and the history of the earth come together in such strong and simple images. And the same extremes exist in drawing: from cave drawings to the computer.

Ken Adam   I was never scared of size, like the volcano, which became the biggest set ever built in this country. It had to be big. And when people ask me why I didn't use

Ken Adam   Ich habe meinen Augen nicht getraut, als ich letztes Jahr in Norman Fosters Architekturbüro eingeladen wurde. Da saßen 600 Architekten am Computer. Es gab kein einziges Reißbrett.

Katharina Fritsch   Manchmal arbeite ich tagelang am Computer, und obwohl ich ausgelaugt bin, habe ich das Gefühl nicht wirklich gearbeitet zu haben. Vielleicht ist es psychologisch. Der Computer ist offensichtlich ein nützliches Gerät und es ist faszinierend, wenn ich meine dreidimensionalen Prints mache. Es ist natürlich spannend, eine bestehende Skulptur scannen und damit herumspielen zu können.

Bice Curiger   In den James-Bond-Filmen gibt es Vulkane, Höhlen, die raue Natur und Steine, die Millionen von Jahren alt sind, und daneben das andere Extrem, die unfassbar hoch entwickelte Technologie, so raffiniert, dass sie bedrohlich wirkt. Technologie, Natur und Erdgeschichte sind in unglaublich starken und einfachen Bildern vereint. Und dieselben Extreme gibt es bei der Zeichnung: von der Höhlenzeichnung bis zur Computergrafik.

Ken Adam   Die Größe hat mir nie Angst gemacht, auch der Vulkan nicht, der das größte je in diesem Land gebaute Filmset war. Es musste groß sein. Und wenn mich die Leute fragen,

a model, I tell them that we couldn't have had 200 stuntmen abseiling from the top. People remember that scene. And then to have a real helicopter flying over the artificial lake. It was the excitement of building something for real. Maybe I was a little crazy.

Katharina Fritsch    It's really great when they crawl down into the crater and throw a stone. The sound it makes, plopping. It's not water, it's not earth and then you see how it glints in the twilight.

Hans Ulrich Obrist    In the early 60s in Japan there was a movement called Metabolism that came up with the idea of a floating city. In their architecture you find a futuristic language combined with biological notions. Where you in touch with these architects, like Kikutake?

Ken Adam    No. Cubby [Broccoli] told me they have a city in Okinawa. So we flew over there to look at it. It looked like an oil rig but it wasn't, and it didn't rise up out of the water, it was stationary. I thought to myself: I flew thousands of miles to see this? Cubby thought I could use it somehow, I worked for nearly a week, trying to make

warum ich nicht ein Modell verwendet habe, sage ich ihnen, dass wir dann nicht 200 Stunt-Männer in den Krater hätten abseilen können. Die Leute erinnern sich an diese Szene. Und dann einen echten Helikopter über den künstlichen Kratersee fliegen lassen. Es war einfach aufregend etwas Lebensechtes zu bauen. Vielleicht war es etwas verrückt.

Katharina Fritsch    Es ist einfach toll, als sie in den Krater runterkrabbeln und einen Stein reinwerfen. Das Geräusch beim Aufschlag. Es ist nicht Wasser, es ist nicht Erde, und dann sieht man, wie es in der Dämmerung schimmert.

Hans Ulrich Obrist    In den frühen Sechzigerjahren in Japan gab es eine Bewegung, die Metabolismus hieß und die Idee einer schwimmenden Stadt propagierte. In ihrer Architektur findet man eine futuristische Sprache in Kombination mit biologischen Ideen. Hatten Sie Kontakt zu diesen Architekten, etwa Kikutake?

Ken Adam    Nein. Cubby [Broccoli] erzählte mir, dass sie eine Stadt in Okinawa hätten. Wir flogen rüber, um sie uns anzuschauen. Sie sah aus wie eine Ölplattform, war aber keine, und sie tauchte nicht aus dem Wasser auf, sondern war starr verankert. Ich dachte mir: Um das zu sehen, bin ich Tausende von Kilometern geflogen? Cubby dachte, ich könnte damit etwas

something work with that structure. I was going crazy. And I threw everything away. Then I came up with this sort of spiderlike structure… And that worked. I also felt relieved because I had moved from straight lines to curved surfaces. It made the construction very difficult – curve upon curve in a fibreglass construction. But it gave me some new design ideas. I was also a little influenced by the French architect, Jacques Couelle, and his utopian visions.

Cristina Bechtler   Yes, he was one of the first architects after the war to design what you might call interactive architecture like the hotel Cala di Volpe in Sardinia. It was all organic forms.

Katharina Fritsch   Like the work of the architect Erich Mendelsohn in the 20s.

Bice Curiger   Yes, the visionary designs of the 20s that Sir Ken mentioned at the beginning of our conversation. It's surprising to discover how many things the two of you share and I'm sure we'd discover more if we continued talking.


anfangen. Ich arbeitete fast eine Woche lang und versuchte etwas Brauchbares auf dieser Basis zu machen. Ich wurde fast wahnsinnig. Dann warf ich alles weg und kam auf diese spinnenähnliche Struktur   Und das funktionierte. Ich war auch erleichtert, weil ich die geraden Linien hinter mir gelassen und zu geschwungenen Oberflächen gefunden hatte. Das erschwerte natürlich die Realisierung – Rundung über Rundung in einer Fiberglaskonstruktion. Aber dadurch kam ich auf neue Gestaltungsideen. Ich stand auch etwas unter dem Einfluss des französischen Architekten Jacques Couelle und seinen utopischen Visionen.

Cristina Bechtler   Ja, er war einer der ersten Architekten nach dem Krieg, der so etwas wie eine interaktive Architektur entwarf, etwa das Hotel Cala di Volpe auf Sardinien. Es bestand ganz aus organischen Formen.

Katharina Fritsch   Wie die Arbeiten des Architekten Erich Mendelsohn in den Zwanzigerjahren.

Bice Curiger   Ja, wie die visionären Formen der Zwanzigerjahre, die Sir Ken am Anfang unseres Gesprächs erwähnt hat. Es ist schon erstaunlich, zu entdecken, wie viel euch beide verbindet, und ich bin sicher, wir würden noch mehr finden, wenn wir das Gespräch noch weiterführen könnten.

# Biographies

Ken Adam, production designer, was born in Berlin in 1921. He moved to London with his parents in 1934 and was a pilot for the Royal Air Force (RAF) during the Second World War. After the war he studied architecture. Ken Adam has been working as a production designer for film productions since the 1950s. He designed countless films including many James Bond movies like *Dr. No* (1962), *Goldfinger* (1964), *Thunderball* (1965) and *You Only Live Twice* (1967) as well as Stanley Kubricks *Dr Strangelove* or: *How I Learned to Stop Worrying and Love the Bomb* (1964) and *Barry Lyndon* (1975).

Cristina Bechtler, publisher, is founder and director of Ink Tree Editions, Küsnacht, Switzerland, an imprint for artists' books, editions and portfolios with contemporary artists. She conceived the book series *Art and Architecture in Discussion*. Previous books in this series have been published with Frank O. Gehry/Kurt W. Forster, Rémy Zaugg/Herzog & de Meuron, Mario Merz/Mario Botta, Jacques Herzog/Jeff Wall/Philip Ursprung, Vito Acconci/Kenny Schachter/Lilian Pfaff, John Baldessari/Liam Gillick/ Lawrence Weiner/Beatrix Ruf, Thomas Demand/Peter Saville/Hedi Slimane/Hans Ulrich Obrist and Ai Weiwei/Uli Sigg/Yung Ho Chang/Peter Pakesch.

Ken Adam, Filmarchitekt, wurde 1921 in Berlin geboren. 1934 Übersiedlung mit den Eltern nach London, im Zweiten Weltkrieg war Ken Adam Pilot für die britische Luftwaffe, nach dem Krieg studierte er Architektur. Seit den 1950er Jahren war Ken Adam Filmarchitekt für Filmproduktionen, unter anderem für die Bondfilme *Dr. No* (1962), *Goldfinger* (1964), *Thunderball* (1965) und *You Only Live Twice* (1967) sowie für Stanley Kubrick's *Dr. Strangelove* or: *How I Learned to Stop Worrying and Love the Bomb* (1964) und *Barry Lyndon* (1975) sowie zahlreiche weitere Filme.

Cristina Bechtler, Verlegerin, ist Gründerin von Ink Tree Editions, einem Verlag für Künstlerbücher, Portfolios und Editionen zeitgenössischer Kunst. Sie konzipiert und realisiert die Buchreihe *Art and Architecture in Discussion*. In dieser Reihe bereits erschienen sind Gespräche mit Frank O. Gehry/Kurt W. Forster, Rémy Zaugg/Herzog & de Meuron, Mario Merz/Mario Botta; Jacques Herzog/Jeff Wall/Philip Ursprung, Vito Acconci/Kenny Schachter/Lilian Pfaff, John Baldessari/ Liam Gillick/Lawrence Weiner/Beatrix Ruf, Thomas Demand/Peter Saville/Hedi Slimane/Hans Ulrich Obrist und Ai Weiwei/Uli Sigg/Yung Ho Chang/Peter Pakesch.

Bice Curiger, art historian and curator, studied art history, ethnology and literary criticism at Zürich University. In the 1970s she worked as an art critic and curator. In 1984 she founded *Parkett* magazine and became its editor-in-chief. Since 1993 Bice Curiger has been working as a curator at the Kunsthaus Zürich where she organized exhibitions like *Birth of the Cool* (1997), *Freie Sicht aufs Mittelmeer* (1997), *Hypermental* (2000), *The Expanded Eye* (2006), and *Katharina Fritsch* (2009). She has been editor of the magazine *TATE ETC.* published by the Tate Gallery in London since 2005.

Katharina Fritsch, artist, was born in Essen in 1956. She studied history and art history in Münster. From 1977 to 1984 she studied at the Kunstmuseum Düsseldorf in the class of Fritz Schwegler. Since 2001 she has been professor for sculpture at the Kunstakademie Münster (Hochschule für Bildende Künste). She has had solo exhibitions at the Kunsthalle Basel, ICA London (both 1988), Dia Center for the Arts, New York (1993), Tate Gallery, London, Museum of Contemporary Art, Chicago (both 2001), Kunsthaus Zürich (2009). In 1995 she received the art prize of the city of Aachen and in 2008 the Piepenbrock prize for sculpture.

Bice Curiger, Kunsthistorikerin und Kuratorin, studierte an der Universität Zürich Kunstgeschichte, Volkskunde und Literaturkritik. In den 1970er Jahren Tätigkeit als Kuratorin und Kunstkritikerin. 1984 war sie Mitbegründerin der Kunstzeitschrift *Parkett*, deren Chefredakteurin sie seither ist. Seit 1993 ist sie feste Kuratorin am Kunsthaus Zürich, wo sie Ausstellungen wie *Birth of the Cool* (1997), *Freie Sicht aufs Mittelmeer* (1997), *Hypermental* (2000), *The Expanded Eye* (2006) und *Katharina Fritsch* (2009) kuratierte. Seit 2005 ist sie Herausgeberin der Museumszeitschrift *TATE ETC.* der Tate Gallery in London.

Katharina Fritsch, Künstlerin, wurde 1956 in Essen geboren. Studium der Geschichte und Kunstgeschichte in Münster. 1977–1984 Studium an der Kunstakademie Düsseldorf bei Fritz Schwegler. Seit 2001 Professur für Bildhauerei an der Kunstakademie Münster (Hochschule für Bildende Künste). Einzelausstellungen unter anderem in der Kunsthalle Basel, ICA London (beide 1988), Dia Center for the Arts, New York (1993), Tate Gallery, London, Museum of Contemporary Art, Chicago (beide 2001), Kunsthaus Zürich (2009). 1995 Kunstpreis der Stadt Aachen, 2008 Piepenbrock Preis für Skulptur.

Hans Ulrich Obrist   was born in Zürich in 1968. He was curator at the Musée d'Art Moderne de la Ville de Paris and has curated many international exhibitions. In 2006 he was appointed Co-Director of Exhibitions and Programmes and Director of International Projects at the Serpentine Gallery, London. His prolific publications on contemporary art include *The Conversation Series, Do it, dontstopdontstopdontstopdontstop* and *A Brief History of Curating*.

Hans Ulrich Obrist   wurde 1968 in Zürich geboren. Er war Kurator am Musée d'Art Moderne de la Ville de Paris und hat weltweit eine Vielzahl von Ausstellungen kuratiert. Seit 2006 ist er Co-Director, Exhibitions and Programmes and Director of International Projects an der Serpentine Gallery, London. Er ist Herausgeber der Buchreihe *The Conversation Series, Do it, dontstopdontstopdontstopdontstop, A Brief History of Curating* und zahlreicher weiterer Publikationen.

List of Illustrations

Previous publications:

-        Mario Botta and Mario Merz
-        Herzog & de Meuron and Rémy Zaugg
-        Frank Gehry and Kurt W. Forster
-        Jacques Herzog and Jeff Wall, moderated by Philip Ursprung
-        Vito Acconci and Kenny Schachter, moderated by Lilian Pfaff
-        John Baldessari, Liam Gillick, Lawrence Weiner, moderated by Beatrix Ruf
-        Thomas Demand, Peter Saville, Hedi Slimane and Hans Ulrich Obrist
-        Ai Weiwei, Uli Sigg and Yung Ho Chang, moderated by Peter Pakesch

In preparation:

-        Frank Gehry and Kurt W. Forster (revised talk)

Series Editor:
Cristina Bechtler, INK TREE, Seestr. 21, CH-8700 Küsnacht
T. +41 44 913 30 99, F. +41 44 913 30 81, www.inktree.ch

© 2009 Springer-Verlag/Wien
Printed in Austria
SpringerWienNewYork is a part of Springer Science + Business Media
springer.at


The publisher and editor kindly wish to inform you that in some cases, despite efforts to do so,
the obtaining of copyright permissions and usage of excerpts of text is not always successful.


Translation from German: Catherine Schelbert, CH-Hertenstein
Translation from English: Suzanne Schmidt, CH-Zürich
Editing: Bice Curiger, Cristina Bechtler, Dora Imhof, Catherine Schelbert
Layout: Michael Karner, www.typografie.co.at
Coverdesign: Walter Zivny, Springer-Verlag, 1201 Vienna
Printing: Holzhausen Druck & Medien GmbH, 1140 Vienna

Printed on acid-free and chlorine-free bleached paper
SPIN: 12653355

With numerous (colored) illustrations

Photo Credits:
Illustrations from the personal archive of Ken Adam, James Bond materials courtesy of EON Productions,
        copyright United Artists (p 14, 15, 16, 18, 19, 20, 21, 24, 25, 26, 36, 46, 52, 54, 55, 57, 79, 81, 86, 87, 88,
        94, 104, 105, 106)
Ivo Faber (p 97)
Katharina Fritsch/ProLitteris (p 32, 33, 39, 44, 45, 50, 51, 61, 66, 67, 69, 70, 71, 73, 74, 75, 77, 84, 89, 92, 97)
Kunstmuseum Basel/Martin P. Bühler (p 74, 75)
Hans Ulrich Obrist (p 10)
Thomas Ruff/ProLitteris (p 84)
Nic Tenwiggenhorn (p 69)
Werner Zellien/ProLitteris (p 32, 33)

ISSN 1613-5865
ISBN 978-3-211-99215-9    SpringerWienNewYork